CW00520656

For those who have served our great country, those that still do, and those who aspire to in the future.

CONTENTS

FOREWORD

In the early days of our relationship my wife interrupted me mid-sentence once, as I began telling a story about one of my good friends from 3 PARA.

"My mate Mick" I started. "He's mad as a box of frogs!"....

Carmen stopped me in my tracks before I got going. "Are any of your mates not mad?" she asked. She'd noticed a recurring theme to my intros.

I'm a very literal person, so I considered her question carefully, quickly thinking through a list of my closest friends. I'd never been asked that before, and never seriously thought about it either, until then.

"No." I answered honestly. "They're all a bit mental."

The general perception of the Parachute Regiment as an aggressive, tenacious, elite group of fearless warriors did not come from nothing; it was earned. Initially on the battlefields of World War Two, and then reinforced on every operation they were deployed on afterwards, from Malaya, to the Falkland Islands, then Iraq and Afghanistan. Over the years men have become legends, and tales of their deeds have become regimental folklore, among the officers and men of the battalions. Inevitably there will be variations in details, and discrepancies in recollections, but the essence of the story, its substance, is what's important. I have chosen to write the stories in this book because they might help people understand what it is like to be a paratrooper in the British Army. The gruelling training that recruits go through, the bond that creates the "Airborne Brotherhood," the exceptional men that make up the ranks, and the absolutely crazy, insane things they will do in the name of fun, loyalty, and honour.

When a group of blokes get together and have a few beers, everyone has amazing stories to tell, and I love listening to them. Over the years I've heard some great anecdotes, told by master orators from my regiment,such as Nick Brown, Steve Bousted, Matt Hellyer, and Eddie Edwards, who could all keep an audience captivated with their animated, hilarious storytelling. Blokes like these can turn a spontaneous "couple of pints" into a night that will be remembered, and talked about for years. I never considered myself as someone who had many stories to tell, until I started writing them down for my first book "You'd be nuts too!"

This book is a collection of stories that have stuck with me over the years. Some because they are funny, and some because they are outrageous. They are all written as they were told to me, or experienced by me, and I have changed or made up many names and places, to either fill a gap in my knowledge, or protect people's confidentiality. Some may well have been exaggerated or embellished by the time I heard them, but I don't really care that much, because I believed them, and I enjoy them. I hope you do too.

CHAPTER ONE

Every Day's A School Day

RUNNING

Early on in recruit training we were out running with our instructors, getting thrashed through a forest on a narrow trail, when the soldier in front of me stopped. Gasping for air, he doubled over, resting his hands on his thighs momentarily, as he tried to control his breathing.

"Come on mate, keep jogging!" I said, as I went past him. Behind me an angry corporal snapped. "Paratroopers don't fucking jog!" he shouted, "Paratroopers fucking run!" he continued emphatically. "Now close the gap and catch the man in front Brown. Work hard, drive on, get fucking up there now!"

There was no time for helping anyone else, it was survival of the fittest, and a word of encouragement was all people would get. We had to concentrate on our own performance, and every day more people would fall by the wayside through injury, inability, or resignation. The corporal was right though, the word jogging was not an accurate description of how we moved. Jogging implies a steady, gentle, sociable activity, with a heart rate below 180 beats per minute, and we did not do that! We ran everywhere, and we ran everywhere really fast, uphill, downhill, through mud, water, or snow.

There were several other things that paratroopers didn't do. We were told in no uncertain terms:

-   **Ironing** – "Paratroopers don't just iron their kit, civvies and the non-ferocious people do that! Paratroopers press it!"

- **Moving at the speed of ten gazelles** – This is the speed everyone else moves at when they're in a hurry. We were regularly ordered to do things "At the speed of a thousand Gazelles!" Much faster than everyone else.

- **Speak to people from other units** – Recruits from other regiments were strictly off limits. Male or female, they were highly infectious to us, and their inferior skills could spread like a virus throughout our platoon if we got close enough, or worse still, spoke to them.

There were also many words that shalt never be uttered by the paratrooper that we were warned about, including:

- **"Squaddie"** – This horrendous slang term for a soldier, used extensively by the British public, media, and most other soldiers, will cause the paratrooper to release a small amount of vomit into his own mouth. Cases of anaphylaxis have been recorded as a result of exposure to this disgusting word. Calling a paratrooper this is extremely offensive, and acknowledged by the judicial system as aggravated assault, where self-defence techniques may be used to protect the afflicted soldier.

- **"Scran"** – This crude alternative to "Scoff" is unacceptable language that is commonly used by soldiers from other regiments and Royal Navy personnel. Paratroopers from northern England that have been exposed to, or even used this word prior to their indoctrination must purge it from their vocabulary and replace it with "scoff" immediately.

- **"Gat"** – For reasons unknown to the airborne community, some soldiers call a rifle, or weapon, a "gat." Even the weapon itself is repulsed by this and will begin to rust and have multiple stoppages in the hands of its owner in a protest of outrage.

- **"Toilet paper"** – Using terminology like this is completely non-aggressive, effeminate, and risks you being mistaken for a civilian. It's "shit-paper!"

- **"Sleeping bag"** – The bag that you sleep in shall never again be called a sleeping bag. Civilians who drive Volvos, use umbrellas, and go camping call it this. "It's a doss bag!" To be fair we didn't get the opportunity to sleep in them much anyway.

SWIMMING

The first time I ever went swimming in the Army was co-incidentally the first time I ever thought I was going to drown. We got thrashed in that pool, and swallowed so much water between us I'm surprised it wasn't empty by the time we finished. We swam a length as fast as we could, climbed out, then ran, crawled, or jumped our way back to the start and went again. After a while, the instructors told us all to stop, and for a moment we thought it was the end. It wasn't. Splitting us in half they took about twenty blokes to the shallow end, and the remainder stayed at the deep end. The blokes at the shallow end got in the water, and to the shouts of "in!" and "out!" they pushed and pulled themselves in unison away from the wall and back, creating an impressive, improvised wave machine. The exercises began once more, this time in a simulated sea-state eight. Not the best swimmer, after a few laps I was exhausted and starting to take on water, my arms hardly lifting on each stroke. I tried to do breaststroke a couple of times to catch my breath, but the instructors were on the pool edge screaming at us to go faster so I carried on, flailing pathetically. Two of the Corporals had jumped in the water to encourage us, and I remember seeing my Section Commander in between waves. He reached out to me, and I actually thought he was trying to give me a hand because I was coughing and obviously struggling. Instead he put both hands on the back of my neck and pushed me under. I couldn't believe it! After what seemed a long time but was probably only a few seconds he let me go, and I got past him as fast as I could., suddenly finding the energy to go fast again. That was, without doubt, the hardest swimming session I've ever done.

During my Physical Training Instructor course we completed the Army Unit Lifesaver Award so that we could supervise swimming sessions back in our battalions. At the end of one lesson our instructor told us to hold our breath under water for as long as we could. He timed us and we all popped up at different times, ranging between twenty to sixty seconds. Once we we'd all resurfaced he instructed us to do it again, but this time using a simple breathing technique. Instead of submerging with full lungs, he said to exhale a small amount of air just before holding our breath and ducking under. It was a mixed result, but most people seemed to improve their time by a little bit. When the last person appeared he told us to get out, and then gave a quick summary of the class before sending us off to the changing rooms. As we walked off to the showers we were startled by a sudden roar from the pool and spun around to see someone still in the water, ripples moving away from where he'd exploded upwards. It was one of the Gurkhas on the course, and he'd been underwater all that time, somehow holding his breath for several minutes, but pushing himself to the limit in the process. He was gasping for air desperately and frantically doggy-paddled to the side to hold on. We all laughed in disbelief, he was a nutter!

Another feat of underwater breath holding and composure I witnessed happened when I was still quite new in battalion. A young soldier called Lee, from the latest intake of recruits had annoyed some of the senior blokes whilst on exercise, and they plotted a suitable response. I don't know what he'd done wrong, probably something heinous like removed both of his boots at the same time or made a brew and not shared it around. The problem was, the blokes were bored, and he was a crow, no further justification was required, he was getting it! At the time we were sheltering in an abandoned warehouse on an old industrial site, waiting to receive orders for the next mission. Lee had cleaned his rifle and eaten his rations before getting into his doss-bag for some rest. Once they were happy he'd nodded off the blokes crept up stealthily and a couple of them jumped on top of him so he couldn't move. Another quickly pulled on the drawcord of the Gore-Tex outer shell and hastily tied a knot, encapsulating him securely. Struggling to pick him up as he wriggled violently, the blokes carried him outside, returning shortly afterwards without him, laughing loudly. About thirty seconds later to everyone's surprise, Lee also returned, completely soaked from head to toe and looking pretty pissed off. I asked someone what had happened.

"We threw him in the water tank. Fuck knows how he got out!" they answered, looking genuinely puzzled. The site had several large, free-standing water reservoirs that were similar in size to a swimming pool, but only three or four feet deep.

I walked over to Lee to check on him. I'd only spoken to him a few times but got on well.

"You alright mate?" I asked.

"Fucking pricks threw me in the water tank in my doss bag!" he said angrily.

I asked him how he'd got out and he produced a pen knife from his pocket. "Luckily, I had this! I cut myself out."

I don't know what the plan was to get him out, or if they even had one, maybe they thought he would just stand up and hop out. It was only supposed to be a prank, but that could have gone horribly wrong.

When you go to Belize with the Army you normally get to do some adventure training or take a few days leave during the trip. One of the popular destinations is a small Caribbean Island called San Pedro which is easily accessible by boat from the mainland and has plenty of cheap accommodation, beautiful beaches, and places to eat and drink. A popular tourist attraction is a place called "Shark Ray Alley" where you can go swimming with Nurse Sharks and Stingrays and a few of my mates wanted to go there when I went with 3 PARA. I didn't! Who the hell wants to swim with sharks!? Plus one of our other mates had already been stung by a Stingray on his adventure training. I went along with it anyway and we set sail on a small excursion boat to a site the tour operator liked. To attract the animals, the captain threw a few bucket loads of fish heads and guts overboard, and within a few minutes we were surrounded by them. Using the snorkelling kit on the boat the blokes started getting in and swimming around, but I sat back and watched for a bit to see if anyone got eaten. To me a shark was a shark, they all looked the same, and I doubted the vicious ones cared if they were invited or not. All of a sudden though, it seemed everyone else was a shark expert.

"Nurse Sharks' teeth are right at the back of their mouths. You'd have to put your hand right in up to the elbow to get bitten." I was assured. "Stingrays won't hurt you. It's only the barbs on the tail that are dangerous." Was the other advice. Everyone was having a good laugh, and nobody was getting chunks taken out of them, so I got in the water and joined in. The water was shallow enough to swim to the floor and I deliberately tried to keep away from the shoals of fish, sharks, and rays. I also stayed close enough to the boat so I could get back on quickly if a Great White or Hammerhead turned up. Before departing we'd chipped in and bought a waterproof camera to get some photos, it was an old fashioned, wind-on, disposable camera, well before everyone had mobile phones or digital cameras. I resurfaced from a dive to the sound of my mate Danny shouting.

"Steve, get a photo, quick!" he called from behind me.

Turning around to face him the camera landed right in front of my face, and I grabbed it quickly before looking across to Danny. To my horror he was bear hugging a fucking shark, and the shark quite clearly didn't like it, thrashing around wildly to escape. It wasn't exactly Jaws, but at about five feet long, it was big enough.

"Let it go you silly fucker!" I said.

"Get a phot! Get a phot!" he insisted excitedly. Anyone would have thought he'd never wrestled a shark before!

I took a photo, wound it on rapidly, then took another.

"Done. Now let it go you lunatic!" I said.

Danny was smiling broadly. "Do you want it? I'll get one of you!" he offered.

"No I fucking don't want it!" I replied.

I never did see those photos.

CRAZY CAMPING

The first time I ever slept out on a military exercise I couldn't even work out how to get into my doss bag. I annoyed the other bloke under my shelter with my fidgeting and banging around, as I naively tried to get into it while it was still folded in half and secured with toggles. By the time I eventually got into it I was sweating and very agitated. Along with the rest of the recruits in my Depot platoon, I'd been issued an old, green, 1958 Pattern doss bag, and shown how to pack it and use it by my corporal, but in the unfamiliar surroundings of the dark forest, I was like a fish out of water. I think the exercise was called "First Try" and it was conducted on a training area close to camp. We were shown how to erect a shelter from a green waterproof poncho sheet and green bungees, how to dig a latrine or "shit-pit" with our green folding shovels, and how to look after our feet with the small, green, plastic foot powder bottle. Ration packs were explained in detail, and we were shown the airborne way to cook them in our issued mess tins. Apparently, soldiers from other regiments would heat up the tins of bacon grill, steak and kidney pudding, baked beans, and other such delights, while still in the tin, by placing the whole thing in boiling water. This type of heinous behaviour was unacceptable in the Parachute Regiment, where everything was emptied into the mess tin and cooked properly. Cooking this way obviously made a mess, but we were taught to clean it up with minimum water, using grass or moss as a scouring pad. That mess tin had multiple uses; we cooked our food in it, made brews in it, washed in it, and even shaved in it. Despite this it was always expected to be immaculate when inspected, a dirty mess tin would mean you were "gungy" and gungyness would not be tolerated. In the ration packs was also some toilet paper or "shit-paper" which actually looked and felt more like grease-proof or tracing paper and was not particularly efficient in its job. Recently, I saw a social media post by a Para Reg legend called Ned Kelly that said issued toilet paper was "like John Wayne......It didn't take any crap from anyone!" To accompany the shit-pit demonstration, one of our corporals demonstrated how to use the shit-paper too. Dropping his trousers, he steadied himself on the shovel behind him and squatted over the small hole he'd dug. Narrating matter-of-factly throughout, he accurately took a crap into the hole, wiped his ass with the issued sheets, stood up, fastened his trousers, then filled the hole back in with earth.

"Any questions on how to take a crap in the field?" he asked the audience of about forty young men.

There were no questions. Not only was the demo very thorough and informative, I think most of us were stunned into silence. I for one had certainly never seen another person do that in public before.

That night, sat around a fire, our instructors soon became bored and started calling people out to tell jokes or to ask them embarrassing questions. Some of the recruits were super confident and got a good laugh from the crowd, especially the older lads in their mid-twenties, but I was dreading the thought of being nominated. I'm one of those annoying people who can remember the punchline to your joke, but can't remember any when put on the spot to tell one of their own. I sank into myself, keeping my head down, and avoiding eye contact. A couple of recruits were given nicknames that night; Private Bullock became known as "Bollocks," Private Bennett became "Tommy" and Private Brooke became "Brook with an E" to differentiate him from the other Private Brook. Despite my pathetic and blatantly obvious attempt to become invisible, I was summoned to perform.

"You!" I heard, and looked up to see the Platoon Sergeant pointing right at me. "What's your name?" he asked.

"Private Brown Sergeant." I answered.

"Stand up and tell us all a joke." he ordered.

My mind went blank as I stood up with everyone watching. There was an awkward silence as I stood there wracking my brains.

"I don't really know any Sergeant." I mumbled embarrassingly.

He was having none of that. "Bullshit, everyone knows a joke, get on with it!" he commanded.

He was right, I did know a joke, but unfortunately the only one I could remember was from a Christmas cracker the year before. I don't know why, but it was genuinely the one single joke I could access in my racing brain.

"Why did the boy eat the fifty pence piece?" I said loudly.

Everyone already looked disappointed, there was no way it was going to be funny. A brief pause followed.

"Because it was his dinner money." I concluded, and although tumbleweed is native to North American deserts, I'm sure a ball of it rolled past me at that very moment, accompanied by the sound of a tolling church bell.

"Sit down!" was the only response from my sergeant, shaking his head glumly.

I'm not the only clueless person to join the army though. A friend of mine was a corporal in Depot, and he told me how he'd found one of his recruits sleeping in a shallow trench, completely submerged in water, with just his head sticking out. Tam had caught the young lad the night before sleeping beside his "shell-scrape" instead of in it. The recruit told him that it was wet and muddy from the rain, but Tam explained that it was better to get a bit wet than get shot by the enemy or hit by shrapnel, and the recruit dutifully returned to the safety of his shell scrape. Returning to check on him in the morning Tam was horrified to find him underwater, wrapped up in his doss bag and its Gore-Tex bivi bag. During the night, the heavy rain had continued, slowly leeching into the man-made sump, and eventually filling it, but because he'd been told off, he dared not get out. Tam rescued him and got him straight to the medical centre to check him over for hypothermia.

I remember my first night of torrential rain in a shell-scrape. I was the section 2IC, or second-in-command for our first tactical exercise in Depot, and one of the jobs the 2IC does is write the "stag list." This is the list that informs everyone what time they are on sentry duty / "stag", which normally consists of lying on a soaking wet floor, in the pouring rain, staring into darkness. The primary job of the sentry is to act as early warning of an enemy attack, while the other soldiers carry out battle preparation or sleep, and there are always two soldiers on stag at a time, so that one of them can leave the sentry position to wake up the next person on duty. While I was writing the stag list my shell-scrape partner, Private Barnes returned from an errand.

"What are you doing?" he asked me.

"Writing the stag list." I replied in a whisper. I'd purchased a waterproof notebook and some marker pens from the NAAFI shop, but quickly realised that the only thing that works when rainwater is dripping from your nose, and your hands are soaking wet is pencil. The red, blue, black, and green markers pens we'd all bought, as according to the packing list, were useless in the rain, and so were the ballpoint pens. Fortunately, the packing list also said "Pencil (sharpened both ends)."

I remember one recruit had bought one of those pencils with an eraser attached to the top. His logic seemed sound, two tools in one, but the corporal wasn't impressed.

"You can't sharpen a rubber you mong!" He said, snapping the tiny rubber off. He then broke the remainder of the pencil in half, before handing it all back to the recruit. "Now you've got two pencils and a rubber. Make sure they're both sharpened at both ends by the next time I see you!" he ordered. It made sense.

My partner had just been helping our section commander, Corporal Fletcher, collect some rations and ammunition.

"Corporal Fletcher said we're not doing stag tonight." Barnes told me.

I was surprised to hear that, we'd had someone on stag the entire exercise. "Really? What did he say?" I queried.
Barnes explained. "He said the weather was too bad, so everyone should stay under their shelters tonight for safety."
I looked around the triangular harbour area, it was dark, and nobody seemed to be moving about.
"Are you sure he said that?" I confirmed. "Nobody is stagging on tonight?"
Barnes was already getting his doss bag out. "The corporals are going to wake us up in the morning. Get your head down while you can." he replied.

Sometimes when an alarm goes off in the morning, you are already half awake, and waiting for it. Other times you sleep right through it because you have selected a peaceful, melodic tune. As a recruit in Depot, you are guaranteed, at least once during every exercise, to be awoken by the sound of gunfire, explosions, flares, and screaming corporals, as your harbour position is attacked by a nominated "enemy force."
Shots of blank 5.56mm rounds and furious shouts of "Where's the fucking sentry!?" and "Why are you fuckers still sleeping!?" woke me up that morning, accompanied by the unmistakeable, muffled sound of people getting kicked while in their doss bags. I sat up and got out of my doss bag so fast it was like I'd been teleported, it was immediately obvious that my section was the only one not awake and returning fire to the assaulting enemy. Frantically we tried to pack away our kit, between firing shots at the advancing soldiers heading our way through the forest, but there was no time.
"Bug out! Bug out!" the corporals shouted over the noise, ordering us to withdraw.
Gathering our kit, we ran after our section commander as he led the way towards the emergency rendezvous point. Like the man in front of me, I was also carrying my sleeping mat as I ran, unable to roll it up and pack it in time in the chaos, and like the man in front I had it ripped from my grasp by our furious Platoon Ser-

geant as I went past him.

"Is that an important piece of fucking equipment is it?" he screamed rhetorically as we carried on running.

Luckily for me the instructors found out about what Barnes had said and didn't punish the rest of us, he however got beasted up and down a hill so much, he quit. For a while I thought that was it for me. I was sure I'd be held responsible, even thinking I might be thrown out of the platoon. I was absolutely devastated, but fortunately my section commander had recognised my enthusiasm, and also noticed Barnes' slack attitude and untrustworthiness.

ANGRY CORPORALS

In Depot there seemed to be times when our instructors were even angrier than normal, for no apparent reason. I don't know whether it was a pre-planned exercise, or if they were genuinely upset about something, but whichever it was, the result was the same; we got beasted, extra beasted. One day we were out running on the Catterick training area and the PTI's were screaming at us.

"You fuckers are not working!"

"Some of you crows are coasting!"

"If you mongs don't start switching on you are gonna be out here all fucking day!"

"You bluffers better start sparking!"

As far as I could tell, everyone was working. All the unfit people had been weeded out by that point, and we'd all kept up with the PTI at the front. Suddenly we were brought to a halt and lined up at the side of the track, jogging on the spot. One of our PTI's walked off and the other began berating us.

"You ungrateful fuckers need to start screwing the nut!" he snarled. Pointing to the other Corporal he carried on angrily.

"Corporal Wakeham has dedicated his life to getting you lot through your training. He spends so much time working for you, his wife has fallen out with him. He has put you crows before his own family because he loves our Regiment and wants you to succeed. His marriage is breaking down because of you!"

We were shoulder to shoulder, in one straight line, facing the track, and he was pacing up and down it menacingly. The more he spoke, the more aggressive he got, and within a few seconds his fists were clenched, and the veins in his neck bulged as he screamed at us. Still shouting, he punched one of the blokes in the stomach, causing him to stumble backwards and fall into the drainage ditch behind us, then did the same to a couple more recruits, he randomly selected. Rant over, the chosen few dusted themselves off and we all formed up on the track in three ranks. Corporal Wakeham took his place at the front and led the way back to camp, extremely fast and via several hills and deep puddles.

The next day when we paraded for fitness our PTI's were seething. We had inadvertently got them in trouble with the Headquarters Staff and needed to be taught a lesson. Forestry workers had witnessed the previous day's events on the training area and reported the unprovoked assault of three recruits. It hadn't taken long to work out who the guilty party was, and our corporals had been reprimanded.

"You fuckers have got us in the shit!" they told us. "If you can't take a little beasting, you're in the wrong regiment!"

It had nothing to do with us, nobody had complained, we wouldn't dare.

"We'll decide how to run your training, not some fucking civvy with a chainsaw, and we've got plenty of other ways to toughen you up!" they stated menacingly.

Off we went for another beasting, but to be honest I don't think it was any harder than what we were accustomed to. It wasn't really possible to make it any harder, everything was already horrendousness level 10 anyway.

Our instructors received a telling off on a few other occasions after complaints from the wives on the married quarters. Sometimes we'd leave camp early in the morning to go for a long tab, exiting the back gate and passing through the housing estate before the Sun was even up. Wearing the old Combat High boots and carrying bergans on our backs, our footsteps would echo off the walls in the dark streets. Our Corporals would encourage us to stamp our feet as hard as we could into the tarmac roads, running slowly but deliberately to his timing.

"Left right, left right, left right, left!" he'd shout loudly, as our hard rubber soles slammed into the ground in unison.

One of our instructors would then call out. "What d'you wanna be?"

"Paratroopers!!" We'd shout aggressively.

Another call would come. "Who do we hate?"

"Hats! Hats! Hats!" Was the well-rehearsed response.

Curtains would be drawn back, and angry wives, woken from their sleep would glare through the windows as we went past, arrogant, and proud in equal measure. It felt great that we were out doing fitness, while the soldiers from other regiments were still sleeping.

Words Of Command

Command from instructor	Meaning	Action by Crows	Reason
"Body!"	The instructor wants a volunteer immediately	Run to the instructor at the speed of a thousand Gazelles and stand at attention	Deliver a message to someone. Make a brew. Get sent to the NAAFI for biscuits (you're buying).
"Corridor!"	Everybody get in the corridor in one straight line, standing to attention	Get in line in the corridor as fast as humanly possible before the instructor shouts the next order	Receive brief. Receive bollocking. Receive mail. Snap inspection.
"From the left, number!"	Starting with the left-hand man, number-off, and do it loudly	Scream the next number up from the man to your left. Just add one, and shout. Quickly, and loudly. Like counting	Anyone not in line by the time the last recruit has shouted his number, is in the shit
"Outside!"	Everybody get outside the building yesterday	Get outside now. Don't stop for anything. If the man in front falls over, run over him. Do not be last.	The instructors want to take you to a different location.
"Three ranks, go!"	Stand in three straight lines	Stand in three, perfectly straight lines both horizontally and vertically	Preparing to march or run somewhere as a group
"Two ranks, go!"	Stand in two straight lines	Stand in two, perfectly straight lines both horizontally and vertically	As above, but through a narrower space or along a busy road
"Hollow square, go!"	Stand in three lines that from above, looks like a square, with one side removed	Stand in three equal straight lines that from above, looks like a square, with one side removed	Kit inspection Receive brief

"Standby!"	Threat of impending punishment	Brace yourself. Keep on your toes. Expect the unexpected	You've angered the instructor and he wants you to suffer some anxiety in anticipation of your punishment
"Standby!"	Get ready. A bit like "On your marks, get set…"	Prepare to do something you don't really want to do, like jump off something high up, or eat some lard	One last moment to psyche yourself up / prepare for action
"Go!"	Move / execute order	Execute order now	Part of your indoctrination conditioning you to react to commands instantly. Preparation for assaulting enemy positions and jumping out of airplanes

Misleading Statements

Statement by instructor	Situation used	Implied outcome	Reality
"It pays to be a winner!"	During P.T or random beastings	If you win a race or event, you'll be rewarded. Maybe you'll get some rest.	It doesn't pay. It just highlights that you are capable of winning, and from now on you will be expected to win everything or be accused of coasting.
"Work for me, and I'll work for you!"	During P.T, random beastings, on exercise, and during inspections	Putting in the graft will convince your instructor to go easy on you	He doesn't work for you! You are a Crow!
"Some of you are not working!"	At any time, regarding anything	People are bluffing, and it might be you. Bluffers get beasted	Everyone is working, but now everyone is paranoid that the instructor thinks they're a bluffer
"You're in your own time now!"	When given a task to do unsupervised	Showing integrity and grafting unsupervised will be rewarded	There is no such thing as your own time when you're a recruit. The instructor is just sick of the sight of you and has something better to do
"Skin is waterproof!"	When it's raining on exercise / In the field	Repeatedly getting soaked to the skin for elongated periods of time, in extreme weather does you no harm	You will get arthritis at an early age and have multiple cold weather injuries because of your service
"The Locker Monster has been!"	When a locker has been left unsecured and unsupervised	Someone's equipment has been ransacked by a mysterious beast that attacks and steals from lockers	In a frenzied rush to get outside, someone forgot to lock their locker and the corporals have destroyed it. Hours of cleaning and ironing may lie ahead to get it back to standard

HYDRATION

In Depot Para you are taught to always fill your water bottles to the very top. The same goes for any water container really, and it's to ensure you get as much of the life-saving fluid as possible into the equipment you carry. During inspections and before exercise instructors will order recruits to show their water bottles. Lids are removed carefully, and bottles are held out for the corporals or sergeants to check. Any recruit found with a bottle not filled to the absolute brim receives the command.
"Over your head!"
He will pour the bottle over himself and stand there wet and cold until directed to go and refill it, properly this time. Sometimes before going for a run, when we wouldn't be carrying water, we'd have a water parade. Lining the corridor, we'd all present our issue black mugs, full to the top with a pint of water. On command we'd drink the entire pint before sprinting outside to begin the run. I hated that, the water would slosh around in my bloated stomach, giving me a stitch, or making me throw up as we got beasted.

Dehydration was not a good excuse to offer instructors in Depot if you underperformed during fitness. In a different recruit platoon from mine one young man tried it, and as a result was ordered to drink a jerry can of water. Military jerry cans hold twenty litres, and to teach him a lesson his corporal made him keep drinking it to the point where he was vomiting after every mouthful. I don't know how much he got through, but I bet he never did that again. Another recruit was put into a bath of cold water and told he couldn't get out until he'd drunk it dry. Apparently he was in there for about an hour before they let him out.

During my time as an instructor at the Survival, Evasion, Resistance and Extraction (SERE) School I was lucky to meet some amazing people from many different backgrounds, but one of the most impressive and inspirational was a man called Dave Sharp B.E.M. Dave was invited to be a guest speaker and give a presentation to SERE specialists from all over the world at the annual SERE Symposium in 2015, and because he was a former paratrooper, I was asked to host him during his visit. From the second we met in the Officers and Sergeants Mess in RAF St. Mawgan, we got on great, like airborne brothers often do. He was more than twice my age, and easily had more than twice my stories that he could recount with amazing detail, despite their vintage and his advanced years. Captured by the Chinese army during the Korean war, he spent two years as a prisoner of war in North Korea, most of which in solitary confinement. Dave's stories that involved water were well beyond anything I'd ever heard, and included a torture method where he was tied to a post outside in the freezing cold, and had cold water poured over his bare feet. He said the pain was terrible and the water would turn to ice, melting momentarily when fresh water was poured over them at random intervals. A very humble man, he made a point of insisting he was not a hero, even though he never surrendered any information to his interrogators and torturers throughout his captivity. One day, I was driving Dave to the train station at Bodmin Parkway, when he was telling me about how he could only eat small amounts of food ever since his imprisonment.
"Why's that mate?" I asked him. "Did your stomach shrink from the starvation?" I knew he didn't mind me asking, he talked openly to me about his ordeal.
"No it wasn't the starvation Steve." He replied. "It's all the scar tissue in my stomach."
He wasn't fishing for a reaction, it was just how he spoke about it, like it was normal conversation. I was intrigued though.
"How do you get scar tissue on your stomach Dave?" I said.

He explained how the Chinese soldiers used to tie him to a chair, force a tube down his throat and into his stomach, then pump him full of water.

Dave was the very last prisoner to be released by the Chinese at the end of the Korean war. He died aged 88 years old, on Remembrance Sunday, 13th November 2016 while staying in the Mess at RAF St. Mawgan, Cornwall. Ironically, he was supposed to be guest of honour at the Newquay remembrance parade, but never made it.

RIP Dave. Actual, real-life LEGEND.

Major Dave Sharp BEM

GRAFFITI

As recruits in Depot, we were taught that paratroopers did not do graffiti. The non-ferocious people did that, not us. We were told that every camp we'd visit in the army would have something derogatory written on the toilet walls or doors about our regiment. Some insecure or jealous individual would cowardly scrawl something pathetic to make themselves feel better. "Do you know what you will never see though?" our corporal asked us. "You will never see anything written back in response. Because we don't do that shit!" He wasn't far wrong. Whenever there is stuff written on the back of the toilet doors in a barracks or a portaloo on a military training area, some spineless wimp has usually written:

"Two things fall from the sky, bird shit and paras." or,

"Para Para in the sky, living proof that shit can fly."

Boring!

Only once in 27 years did I see a comment in response, and although I was gutted, I had to admit it was quite funny.

Written beneath the "Para Para in the sky" rhyme in a red-hot, claustrophobic portaloo in the Kuwait desert was:

"Craphat craphat in the gutter, kicked to death by an airborne nutter!"

Drawing in each other's notebooks was always alright though and leaving one unattended was a schoolboy error. We'd spend ages leaving long messages to one another, sometimes with only one word per page. My mate Scotty ruined an entire notebook of mine like that once, letting me know how gay I was, how much of a slut my girlfriend was, and what a pathetic excuse for a paratrooper I'd become.

An officer friend of mine was snapping when he took out his notepad to take notes, and found cocks drawn all over it. His main issue was that it was during a brief from the brigade commander, who wasn't impressed. Maybe it's an age thing, but I never saw the comedy in drawing penis's everywhere like you see nowadays though. No doubt I would have done it in my younger days, but as a sergeant major I had a sense of humour failure with the blokes over it one day.

About the same time as the officer's notebook incident, we were having a visit by some other officers from the battalions, and I was having a quick walk round to make sure the place was tidy. On entering one of the offices I was confronted with a modern art masterpiece, in the form of a giant, spurting penis on the floor, made out of white mine tape. I took a deep breath and closed the door, our guests were due in five minutes. With a new found sense of urgency I checked the rest of the offices and classrooms, and in one of them I found another similar depiction, this time drawn in black marker pen, on a free-standing whiteboard. Whoever did it was indeed a gifted artist, it had veins, pubic hair and of course an impressive amount of ejaculate. I didn't take the time to breathe or shut the door this time, immediately storming into the Interest Room where the blokes were sitting.

"Right you fuckers, whoever's been drawing cocks all over the building needs to get rid of them in the next sixty seconds, or I'm going to fucking lose my shit!" I snapped. "If you lot like cock so much, get a fucking boyfriend! It stops now! No more drawing cocks in notebooks, no more cocks in offices, and no more cocks on whiteboards! Fucking enough!"

No doubt the blokes had a good chuckle once I left and took the mickey out of the grumpy old man, but they tidied up and nothing more was said. That evening, I was driving through camp and as I turned a corner, the setting Sun beamed straight into my eyes, impairing my view. Reaching up instinctively, I grabbed the visor above my head and lowered it. Low and behold, on the back side of that visor, drawn with a ballpoint pen, was another spurting penis. That was probably the only time I saw the funny side of that graffiti. I bet the blokes would have paid good money to see that. Bastards!

MY MATE GINGE

One of my many good friends in 3 PARA called Ginge had a natural gift for winding people up, really getting under their skin. We were close friends and served in battalion and Pathfinders together, but even I got wound up to snapping point by him once. He was in my bunk, a small, single-man room, and chopsing off about something and I'd had enough.

"Ginge, fuck off, you're pissing me off now!" I said.

He custard pie'd me straight away, and continued pressing my buttons, either not realising, or not caring that I was genuinely snapping.

I'd had enough. "Seriously Ginge, get out before I punch you in the fucking head!" I growled.

His response was so unbelievably irritating, and so dismissive, that instead of being angry I just burst out laughing.

"Yeah, cos you can like, cos you would like, cos you will, won't you!?" he said rapidly. He didn't give a monkey's.

In Depot, Ginge's abilities were identified by his instructors early on in training. One day, noticing a Corporal from another Regiment taking his recruits through a lesson outside, his Section Commander instructed Ginge on what he wanted him to do, and sent him on task. Sat in a semi-circle in front of their Corporal, the recruits listened intently as their instructor delivered his lesson. As a recruit, your Corporal is your idol, your mentor, and your disciplinarian. He is untouchable, beyond reproach. To the Parachute Regiment recruit that level of respect is only afforded to Parachute Regiment Corporals, we were taught from day one that the other Regiments, the non-ferocious, the Craphats, were unworthy of our recognition.

As instructed, under the watchful eye of his Section Commander, Ginge marched proudly towards the lesson, his arms swinging shoulder high, neck back in his collar, and the instructor paused mid-sentence as Ginge halted smartly in the middle of the class. As everyone looked on in stunned silence, shocked by the blatant rudeness of the interruption, Ginge took a deep breath then screamed at the top of his voice.

"I fucking hate hats!!" He then executed a sharp about-turn and marched cockily back to re-join his Section. Nothing happened. I can confidently say that if that had been the other way around, and a Parachute Regiment Corporal was insulted like that, there would have been several hospitalisations.

Ginge's whole Depot Platoon were weaponised once to ruin the passing-out parade of some recruits from another Regiment. What was probably the proudest day of their lives, and also a proud day for their families in the audience was sabotaged by Ginge and his mates, under the direction of their Corporal. During the parade Ginge and the other forty or so Para Reg recruits were deployed by their Corporal to stand on the opposite side of the parade ground to the spectators. Standing behind the spectators, the Corporal had instructed them to react with a chant every time he raised his arm. He waited for the band to stop playing and during a brief pause before the speeches raised his arm. Ginge and co. reacted as briefed. "We hate Hats! We hate Hats!" they yelled in unison until the hand went down. Forty overworked, underfed, aggressive young men with shaven heads chanting like that is a distraction for anyone, and they repeated it a couple more times before returning to the block. Their antics were probably the lasting memory of everyone in attendance. Mission success!

Ginge won a television from a raffle in Depot once, but it was a fix. The Corporals informed the recruits that a T.V was up for grabs at £10 a ticket and everyone bought one. They should have known better, T.V's were not allowed, recruits couldn't even have a poster or photo, and even if they did get a T.V there was no time to watch it anyway. Depot was relentless, from the moment you got up you were under pressure to get things done and permanently on edge, waiting to react to the next command, barked out from the Staff Room. Names were to be drawn out of a helmet (not a hat, because paratroopers don't own, use, or associate with hats.) and Ginge was taken to one side and pre-briefed that his name would be drawn. In reality there were no names in the helmet, just forty blank pieces of paper screwed up tight. Ginge was told to feign surprise and act excited when the winner was announced. He'd be presented the T.V in front of the others, then return it to the staff a few minutes later so the duty Corporal could use it at night.

As briefed Ginge acted ecstatic to be the winner when his name was called out, putting on a good show and legitimising the raffle, then as briefed he returned it to the staff room. Some might say that was theft, others would call it character building.

CLEAR AS MUD

I never stopped learning in the army, which is one of the reasons I stayed so long. There was always an abundance of things to learn and plenty of people with specialist knowledge, skills and experience that they were willing to pass on. Some military terminology is generic across the three services of the Navy, Army, and Air Force and some is service specific, with the Royal Navy having almost an entire language of their own called "Jack Speak." Different regiments and corps also have their own phrases, nicknames, and abbreviations too. Some are geographical dialects, some are historical, and some are private jokes amongst a smaller group. I spent a year in 1 PARA as a Sergeant Major, and quickly learned that they used a lot of language that I'd never heard of. One of the first meetings I attended had so many abbreviations, acronyms, and phrases that I'd never heard before, I didn't even ask for clarification during it. In fact, even the name of that meeting was a new one on me, and when I was told to be at "D and G" at 1400hrs I had to ask what D and G stood for.

"Direction and guidance." I was informed. A few months later it changed to HODS (Heads of departments). It seemed like every other word at D+G was a codeword, stopping to ask would have dragged that first meeting out for hours. Instead, I wrote them down as they were spoken, missing out on most of the information being relayed, with a view of educating myself prior to the next gathering. I walked out of that conference room having learned one thing; I had a lot to learn! After the meeting I collared one of the other sergeant majors who'd been inside and joked about my ignorance to the terminology, hoping he would educate me. He was a Scotsman called Gordy I knew from a course we'd done together, and a great bloke.

"Aye Steve, I didn't understand half of it either mate." he assured me. "Nobody does. Sit with me next time and I'll help you out." That meeting was also the first time I'd heard people referred to exclusively by their job role rather than their name too, according to the MoD responsibility numbering system. That system is detailed below:

Service – Each service has its own single-letter prefix.

A =   Air (RAF)

G =   General (Army)

N =   Navy (Maritime)

J =   Joint services

Topic

1 =   Personnel

2 =   Intelligence

3 =   Operations

4 =   Logistics / Medical

5 =   Planning

6 =   Communications and information systems

7 =   Training

8 =   Finance and Human Resources

9 =   Policy, Legal and Media Operations

These letters and numbers are used to denote an area of responsibility or topic. For example:

A1   = R.A.F personnel

G2/3 = Army intelligence operations

J3/5 = Joint operational planning

The Staff Officer, SO numbering system denotes the rank / authority of the service person with parity across the MoD, due to the different rank structures / titles given to the three armed services and the Civil Service:

	Navy	Army	RAF	Civil Service
SO1	Commander	Lieutenant-Colonel	Wing Commander	Civilian who knows they will never, ever be sacked, no matter how incompetent they are, and will talk to soldiers with total disdain.
SO2	Lieutenant-Commander	Major	Squadron Leader	Civilian who likes to tell you they hold the equivalent rank of Major in the hope you will accept their condescending behaviour. They hold no rank.
SO3	Lieutenant	Captain	Flight Lieutenant	Civilian with good intentions early on. Will rapidly become disillusioned by the slack attitudes of their arrogant, overpaid superiors.

Some people actually introduce themselves and answer the phone by their job role, like SO2J35 or SO3J57. It's a bit like saying you're 007 except it sounds crap, and you come across as a complete tool to everyone outside of your organisation.

The parachuting world also has its own terminology that even as a tandem master with several hundred jumps, I never understood, or felt the need to learn. One thing I heard many times during parachute briefs was the term "strong side of the wind" and it was always talked about like it was really important. The instructor would say things like "Make sure you are on the strong side of the wind, or you won't make it back to the drop zone." or "If you are on the strong side of the wind you will overshoot the DZ." I bet nearly everyone else in those briefs under-stood it just as much as me, but we'd all sit there nodding along in agreement like it made perfect sense. As far as I've ever been able to tell, there is no such thing, there's just wind, and if it's behind you, you go faster, if it's in your face, you go slower, and if it's blowing from the side, you go sideways. I find that if I turn my canopy towards the DZ, that's generally the way I'll go. K.I.S.S - Keep it simple stupid. We used to get loads of information be-fore jumps sometimes, especially high altitude one's. We'd get the windspeed and wind direction at different heights, the tem-perature at different heights, the aircraft heading, the release point location, the landing area location, the location of hazards such as water courses, high structures, mountains, roads, towns and more. All we were interested in was pull height, where the landing area was, and how it was marked. As long as the crew chucked us out in the right place, it wasn't all that complicated really.

Saying that, I was on a jump in America once where the crew dis-patched us in completely the wrong place. During freefall I was unable to identify the DZ, which wasn't all that unusual because the desert all looks the same from high up, but when I deployed my parachute I still failed to see it. Sometimes, especially dur-ing strong winds we'd be dropped a good distance away, but this day wasn't that windy, and I couldn't even see a single vehicle or marker panel anywhere. I was halfway through a slow turn, scanning the ground around me when in the distance I saw an area I recognised. It was the DZ, but not the DZ we were supposed to be jumping onto. I started heading towards it, hoping we had enough altitude to cover the distance, and the rest of the blokes followed on behind me in a straight line. Someone had definitely messed up, because as we got closer it was clearly unmanned. There was no marker, no windsock, no medic, and no DZ Safety Officer, they were all at the other DZ, many miles away, looking skywards, and wondering where we were. It was good though, because we had to work out the wind speed and direction for ourselves and we all landed safely in a nice tight group. No harm done.

CHAPTER TWO

Mindset

WHAT MANNER OF MEN ARE THESE?

"What manner of men are these who wear the maroon beret? They are firstly all volunteers and are then toughened by hard physical training. As a result they have that infectious optimism and that offensive eagerness which comes from physical wellbeing. They have jumped from the air and by doing so have conquered fear. Their duty lies in the van of the battle: they are proud of this honour and have never failed in any task. They have the highest standards in all things, whether it be skill in battle or smartness in the execution of all peace time duties. They have shown themselves to be as tenacious and determined in defence as they are courageous in attack. They are, in fact, men apart, every man an Emperor." - *Field Marshal The Viscount Montgomery of Alamein*

The Parachute Regiment is deservedly famous for its short, but glorious fighting history. Its soldiers are revered across the world for their tenacity and aggression on the battlefield, which they have reinforced every time they've been called upon since their formation in World War Two. Over the decades there have been many times where people have questioned the requirement or relevance of parachute troops in the British army, disputing their employability in modern day warfare. To the paratrooper, the method of insertion is only a small part of the job and does not define the soldier. We will insert by whatever means available or necessary; plane, helicopter, armoured vehicle, four wheels, two wheels, running, walking, crawling, swimming. The blokes will do whatever it takes to close with, and kill the enemy, no matter the odds, no matter the sacrifice. This mentality and adaptability does not come from parachuting, it comes from the individual that is created during Parachute Regiment recruit training, then shaped in the battalions.

Any man who walks into an armed forces careers office and declares that he wants to join the Parachute Regiment has, in my opinion, already shown at least one desirable trait, ambition. Volunteering for the hardest course possible, rather than taking an easier route is a good start. I have met countless people who told me they wanted to be a paratrooper but didn't even try because it was too hard. While at Depot, recruits know that their life can be made infinitely easier, and their pathway to an army career much smoother, by opting to leave or transfer to a different regiment or corps. Those with the requisite determination will resist this temptation, or most likely not even consider it, continuing to embrace the grind. They will get up earlier, work harder, run faster, carry heavier loads, dress smarter, eat quicker, and sleep less than every other recruit they encounter. Many will fall by the wayside during the Depot process, some asking to leave, some failing, some through medical conditions, the occasional bloke will go AWOL. After six months approximately a third will pass the course and be sent to their battalion.

Men capable of enduring the long road to battalion are highly motivated, robust individuals, capable of working in a team, or as an individual under their own initiative, under extreme pressures and circumstances. The aggressiveness and infamous reputation of the regiment can sometimes detract from the calibre of man that makes up its numbers, but within the battalions there is so much talent beyond the soldiering skills. Athletes, martial artists, tradesmen, musicians, academics, artists, farmers, and sportsmen can all be found in the Companies. Most of these men would have excelled at whatever career they'd chosen, but fortunately for the army they chose the Paras. Don't get me wrong though, there's still plenty of absolute nutters too!

One of my mates in 3 PARA was a bloke called Mick, from Middlesbrough. We met on our military skiing instructors course in Norway where we were accommodated in the same room on Bomoen Camp. Mick was quite new to battalion at that point, and I'd never spoken to him before, but when I was doing my push ups on the first night he asked if he could join me. Although fairly small in height, Mick had a very muscular physique, with a tiny waist and huge back and he matched me on the push-up bars easily, both taking turns to complete ten sets of forty. After my last set I stood up and walked towards the door to the corridor as two other soldiers walked past. Stopping in their tracks they stared past me into the room, looking surprised. I turned around to see what they were looking at and saw Mick in a perfect, vertical handstand on the push-up bars. He did a couple of handstand push-ups, then dropped his whole body to a horizontal position and did a couple more, feet still off the ground. I had never seen anything like it, it was amazing to watch. Mick was a gymnast on the GB team before joining the army. Word quickly spread about his awesome talent and the blokes would ask him to perform somersaults and back flips regularly. The only time he failed to deliver was after about ten pints of lager in the Norwegian T.V room. The blokes were performing on top of a few tables that had been pushed together when someone asked Mick to do a back-flip. I was sat with him and told him not to. The tables were all wobbly and so was he.
"You're steaming mate. You'll hurt yourself." I said.
He was having none of it, he'd done it a thousand times before.
"It's alright mate, he slurred, it's easy."
To a rapturous applause he climbed onto the tables in the middle of the room and after gathering himself for a couple of seconds leapt upwards and backwards.
"Ooooh!" Said the crowd in unison as he landed on his head with a loud thud, before bursting into laughter as he stood back up. Mick shook himself off and jumped again.

"Oooooh!" We all said again as he face planted into the wooden surface once more. He wanted to try again, but we talked him out of it, he could have broken the bloody table!

Another friend in 3 PARA who I also went through Depot with was Tiddy. He had the face of a sixteen year old, the body of a twelve year old and the boxing ability of a middleweight boxing world champion. Before the army Tiddy was a schoolboy boxing champion from Manchester and he had the confidence and swagger to go with it. Also in my Depot platoon was a Tae Kwon Do black belt from Scotland called Tam, an Aikido black belt, a bodybuilding champion, a stone mason, a stuntman, an engineer, and a kickboxing champion. We also had a lot of geographical diversity too. Unlike the county regiments, the Parachute Regiment doesn't focus its recruiting on a specific demographic and attracts applicants from all over the United Kingdom and beyond. My Depot platoon had Cornishmen, Londoners, Brummies, Yorkshiremen, Welshmen, Scotsmen, South Africans, and Kiwis, but it meant nothing to anyone; all that mattered was whether or not you were a good bloke, a grafter, a team player.

AIRBORNE
AFICIONADOS

Since its formation on the 1st of August 1942 during World War Two. The Parachute Regiment has become both famous and infamous for its actions on the battlefield, on operations, and in peacetime duties. To its citizens, friends, and allies it represents the elite of the British army, a force to be reckoned with, and a special group of men that can be called upon when acts of extreme violence and sacrifice are anticipated. Few military units will send a shiver down the spine of the enemy when they hear of their impending arrival, but the Paras are definitely part of this class.

Sgt Fleming

When presented with our parachute wings on the drop zone at Weston-on-the-Green, our Platoon Sergeant gave a great speech, where he described the reputation of our chosen cap-badge and what we had to live up to. Talking of the Falklands War, he said: "When the Argentinians heard that the Parachute Regiment, the Royal Marines, and the Gurkhas were coming to fight them, they fucking shit themselves! They had already lost! Because they knew what those soldiers were capable of doing to them! Imagine if they were told it was some other non-ferocious regiments they'd never heard of. They wouldn't have given a shit!" - *Sergeant Fleming PARA, 1993*.

As a recruit it was awesome to become a part of that, and whether or not he was right, it was very inspiring.

Benjamin Franklin

World War Two saw the first large-scale operational use of para-troopers, with the German Fallshirmjager launching assaults in Denmark and Norway before invading Crete with about 14,000 paratroopers. However, the concept had been thought about well before that time. Benjamin Franklin, a founding father of the U.S.A, polymath, inventor, scientist, printer, politician, free-mason, and diplomat wrote the following in 1784:

"Where is the prince who can afford so to cover his country with troops for its defence, as that ten thousand men descend-ing from the clouds, might not, in many places, do an infinite deal of mischief, before a force could be brought together to repel them?" - *Benjamin Franklin, 16 January 1784*

Margaret Thatcher

A soldier who attended the Parachute Regiment 17th Anniver-sary of the Falklands War wrote the following, about a speech given by ex-Prime Minister Margaret Thatcher at the event.

"Wisened with age and looking frail, she took to the stage, paused, and looked us all in the eye. She seem to grow a hundred feet tall as she uttered these immortal words":

"The Parachute Regiment, should be locked up and only be let out in time of war!"
- *Margaret Thatcher, 1999.*

"To us that was the highest compliment anyone could pay us. We lived for the fight, it was part of our ethos. We trained hard so war was easy; we sweated more, so we would bleed less on the battlefield. We set the highest standards, none could follow. We had the most battle honours and awards for outstanding brav-ery than any other Regiment in the British Army since we were formed at the bequest of Sir Winston Churchill. We were born in battle." - *Falklands War Veteran, PARA.*

AIRBORNE
ANTAGONISTS

To its enemies, doubters, and critics, the Paras represent something completely different; Thugs, psychopaths, elitists, an outdated, obsolete force that has no place in modern warfare. Some of these might be true. Some will be seen by the blokes as compliments, and another reason for the enemy to fear them. But, whether you are a friend or foe, there is no denying the operational effectiveness and special capability these soldiers possess. Often, those that attempt to undermine the reputation of the Parachute Regiment by labelling them as mindless, bloodthirsty, maniacs, will achieve exactly the opposite effect amongst the young soldiers in its ranks. While politicians and senior officers will recoil in horror at the latest allegation or indictment, soldiers will celebrate the renewed notoriety; the more outrageous, the better. Newspaper articles will be cut out, and stuck to walls in the accommodation, and social media posts forwarded to everyone on their friends list. Haters inadvertently become unintentional exponents, giving a morale boost to those it seeks to agitate, and further encourage the young men with aspirations to join them:

The Sunday Telegraph
In 1995, following the release of 3 PARA soldier Lee Clegg, the Sunday Telegraph printed a story about the Parachute Regiment called "The Lost Tribe." Clegg had been given a life sentence in 1993 after being found guilty of murder while on duty in Northern Ireland but was released on licence after two years and

subsequently cleared of the charges in 1998. The article gave a mixed review of the Paras; acknowledging their comradeship and courage, but also casting aspersions on their ability to co-exist with, or operate amongst others in a peaceful, responsible manner:

"The 3,000 strong regiment's reputation is part of its combat power. Lesser men should give up and run, just knowing they are faced with the Paras. Argentine conscripts did so on the road to Port Stanley. In much the same way "crap-hats" (as Paras call soldiers without airborne wings) stand aside when confronted in an Aldershot bar. The Para pubs are legendary. If there's no blood on the streets of the Hampshire town on a Saturday night, the regiment is slacking."

Referencing allegations relating to the Falklands War, the article also stated:

"An inconclusive police investigation into claims that Paras shot Argentine prisoners and cut the ears off corpses during the Falklands War sullied the regiment's reputation." – *The Sunday Telegraph, 9 July 1995.*

The Sunday Telegraph

COMMENT

The lost tribe

Kevin Myers

A journalist, writing for the The Independent (Ireland) wrote the following controversial statement about Bloody Sunday: "You would have to be an idiot, psychopath, or militaristic bigot to think that anything other than mass murder occurred on Bloody Sunday, January 30, 1972. But that day was not totally unique: it was merely an extravagant example of what the Parachute Regiment was already doing and would continue to do in Northern Ireland."

He also went on to credit the paras for IRA recruitment:

"The IRA had no better friend than the Parachute Regiment; wherever the Paras went, IRA recruitment subsequently rose." - *Kevin Myers, 16 June 2010.*

Patrick Bury

In 2015 the Irish Times published an article about Bloody Sunday, with the headline: "Paras were the wrong regiment in the wrong place."

The following are excerpts from that story:

"That the elite, aggressive, fighting unit of the British army was used to contain a civil rights demonstration highlights poor judgement at the higher echelons of military command, a failure to recognise the innate ethos of paratroops, and poor tactical leadership by those paratroop leaders on the ground."

"Shock troops require a certain kind of individual, a certain kind of training and a certain kind of ethos. It requires a training programme that triumphs aggressiveness, endurance, decisive action, the maximum use of violence and momentum, and offensive spirit." – *Patrick Bury, 11 Nov 2015.*

The German Army in North Africa

It is commonly thought that the nickname "The Red Devils" came about because of the maroon beret worn by British paratroopers, but this is not the original reason. During the fighting in North Africa, the British 1st Parachute Brigade earned the moniker from their German adversaries because of their appearance when fighting in the reddish mud of the desert, which they were often coated in during battle. It is also said that the trailing tail-piece of the parachute smock reminded the Germans of Lucifer's tail. In German they called them "Rote Teufeln" – The Red

Devils. The name was considered a compliment by the soldiers, and the Commander of British Airborne Forces, congratulated them, saying:

"First Parachute Brigade have been given the name by the Germans of Red Devils. General Alexander (Britain's commander in the Middle East) congratulates the Brigade on achieving this high distinction. Such distinctions given by the enemy are seldom won in battle except by the finest fighting troops." – *General Browning, Commander British Airborne Forces, circa 1942.*

WHO YOU CALLING BRAINWASHED!?

When I attended my Physical Training Instructors course in Aldershot in 1998 I was at the height of my indoctrination. I'd completed a couple of courses with soldiers from other regiments by then, including my promotion course that I'd only just recently finished, and my belief in the superiority of my regiment was strengthened every time. The PTI course had about fifty students on it, with a good percentage from the Parachute Regiment, and we all quickly found each other to form what is known as the "Blood Clot," because of our maroon berets, and the way we stick together. There were men from all three battalions represented, and some extremely fit soldiers. In a lot of army units PTI's are revered as super-athletes, cutting about in their white PTI t-shirts and red belts at every opportunity. In my regiment being a PTI meant nothing, it didn't mean you were the fittest, it just meant that you had passed a course; a course that plenty of soldiers from the non-ferocious regiments had passed. There are lots of blokes in the Para battalions that are outrageously fit, but chose not to, or didn't get the opportunity to do the PTI course. In our battalions you are judged by your deeds, not by your badges. On my course there was a bloke from the Royal Logistics Corps who couldn't run for toffee, and the only dumbbell he'd ever picked up was himself. He had a fat belly, a double chin, and the posture of an arthritic Turkey on Christmas Eve. However, he was a very good swimmer, and could execute a textbook cartwheel on both sides. That bloke was so excited about the prospect of passing the course, he was planning to get a PTI badge tattooed on his arm after the first week. One day while on a load carry, we noticed that he was wearing a para-helmet. Paratroopers and airborne soldiers were issued para-helmets and he was neither. That night we borrowed the helmet and took turns pissing into it until it was filled to the top, and when we returned it to his bedspace one of the blokes drew beards and moustaches on every picture he had put up of his girlfriend and young child. Looking back, as a mature adult, I can see how out of order that was now and understand how people might be repulsed by that disgusting behaviour. I would agree with them .... How dare he wear a para-helmet! Outrageous!

To be fair there were some good blokes and girls on that course from across the army, but after a couple of weeks a few of us started to wind each other up about having "Hat" friends. Working closely in teams from morning till night, doing sports and fitness we inevitably formed friendships with some others on the course, but we decided that anyone caught talking to someone not Para Reg should be punished. The appropriate penalty was determined to be fifty push-ups per incident, which seemed easy enough to avoid until the next morning.

"Morning Steve." Said a commando engineer called Pat, as I walked into the changing room. He was one of the fittest on the course and a decent bloke. I looked across to see if my mate Shaun was watching; of course he was, and he was grinning from ear to ear in anticipation.

"Hello Pat." I replied. Shaun raised his hand immediately with outstretched fingers and mimed the word "fifty!"

I nodded in acknowledgement, I was bang to rights.

We all spied on each other for the rest of the course and kept tallies on who owed what. In the evening we'd meet up in the accommodation and carry out our punishment averaging three or four hundred push ups per night.

In my team there were three of us who were particularly indoctrinated; Si from 1 PARA, Daz from 2 PARA, and me from 3 PARA.
We were obsessed with our regiment, but laid it on extra thick
sometimes, just to wind up the course instructors. During one
lesson in the sports hall, our instructor, a big Staff Sergeant from
the Army Physical Training Corps, asked the question:
"What do we need to do if we want to become the best at some-
thing?"
I knew the answer he wanted, the whole lesson had been about
specific training programmes. I raised my hand to answer.
"Go ahead." He said, nodding towards me.
"You need to join the Parachute Regiment!" I stated confidently.
"What? No, not that." he said, shaking his head in frustration.
"Think about the type of training that will give the best results in
a chosen sport." he clarified.
I feigned ignorance, pretending not to understand and Si called
out with his answer.
"Six months in Depot is definitely the best way to get fitness re-
sults!" he offered.
"No, no. You're missing the point lads." The instructor replied.
"What I'm asking is, what's the best way to ensure your training
is effective for your goals?"
Daz was next. "You make sure every single session is a beasting
from hell that makes you feel sick!"
Our instructor gave up asking. "No, no, no. Guys, the answer is
sport specific training. We need to do sport specific training."
He looked at us with a mixture of frustration and pity, then explained to the other students why we were the way we were.
"The thing is guys, what you have to understand is; these Paras
are different to the rest of us. That is how they actually think, because they are taken away as young men and brainwashed. The
training they do is like nothing we can even imagine, so that's
why they think the way they do."
We'd got into his head.

SYMPATHY? DENIED!

Sympathy from soldiers can be found in the myths and legends aisle, right between rocking-horse shit and hen's teeth. It is neither expected or given, and is usually replaced with sarcasm, humiliation, and mockery. We learned this early on in Depot by observing how the instructors dealt with recruits who struggled physically or psychologically. They were ruthless, pointing out weaknesses or failings for all to see and laugh about. Sometimes making a joke from a situation is actually the best way to deal with it. Not only does it get it out in the open, but it's also hard to feel sorry for yourself when everyone else is making fun of your problem or situation.

When one of the recruits from my platoon was accidentally stabbed in the back of the leg by a bayonet, the corporals were totally unemotional, even though they were the ones who'd given us a lesson on the bayonet and told us how lethal it was. We'd just finished practising rifle drill with bayonets fixed, when we were marched to the accommodation block, halted outside, and ordered to fall out. As always we had two minutes to get in, find our locker keys, change clothes, secure our rooms, and get back outside in three ranks. We sprinted to the door, unloading the magazines from our rifles as we ran, but some still had bayonets fixed as we all got trapped in the bottleneck of the door. In the usual, mad rush, with the corporals screaming "hurry up!" and "Don't be last!" one of the recruits stuck his bayonet into the calf of another bloke. Dropping to the floor, holding on to his leg, McClusky was obviously in a lot of pain, grimacing and looking very worried. Everyone stopped to look when someone shouted, "man down, man down!" and the blood from his wound was clearly visible on the floor. One of our instructors, Corporal Bates was a Falklands War veteran, who'd probably seen a few bayonet wounds before, in battle, and he took charge. Another corporal went straight into the building via the staff entrance to call the Medical Centre.

"Apply direct pressure to the wound!" he ordered clearly, pointing to one of the young men who immediately pressed his hand against the cut. Calmly pointing to another soldier he gave further instructions. "You! Lay him on his back and elevate the leg!" McClusky was obviously scared by the loss of blood and began shouting in pain, but Corporal Bates was having none of that. "Calm down princess, it's just a little scratch. Don't make a scene out of it." He was as cool as a cucumber, and that calmness gave us all confidence that everything was in hand. That is how a real leader acts under pressure. "What are you mongs waiting for?" he asked the rest of us, as we watched on. "You now have one minute, forty seconds to get your admin squared away and back outside in three ranks! Now hurry up! Get away!"

We were back outside quickly, dressed in different clothes and boots, and barely had time to look at McClusky who was still lying on the ground as we ran past once more and carried on with our day. He was taken to hospital, and we never saw him again, unfortunately he didn't make it. He didn't die, he just didn't make it through Depot.

A friend of mine from B Company, 3 PARA was among 44 soldiers injured, when he broke his back on a parachute descent into Sardinia in 1994. The ill-fated jump onto the aptly named "Exercise Dynamic Impact" was conducted during strong winds that many thought were out of limits and resulted in several soldiers being hospitalised. On landing, Danny knew that he was injured and got the attention of another soldier who landed nearby, asking him to fetch medical assistance. Using his radio, that soldier called the headquarters and relayed the message of a casualty. After a short chat he briefed Danny of the outcome.

"You need to grab your kit, and make your way to the Company RV. When you get there the medic will see you." he told him.

Danny was in a lot of pain, and worried about the damage he may have done to his back, but Danny was also a new bloke who'd only been in battalion about four months, so attempted to do as he was told. Gathering his heavy equipment, he agonisingly hoisted it onto his back and began to walk slowly across the drop-zone towards the rendezvous point. Despite a determined effort, his legs buckled, and he fell to the ground, paralysed from the waist down.

Eventually accepting that his injuries were significant, the medics were deployed to his location and Danny was evacuated to hospital for treatment, where he slowly regained the feeling in his legs, and began his recovery. A couple of months later, back in Aldershot, he was up and about, getting stronger every day when he was summoned to see the Company Quartermaster Sergeant (CQMS), who controlled the stores and equipment for B Company. Walking gingerly, he entered the storeroom. The CQMS saw him enter and explained why he'd been sent for.

"I need the clothes that you were issued for Sardinia back." he told Danny bluntly.

Danny was surprised to hear that. "The medics cut them off me on the DZ when I broke my back Colour." he replied. His defence was pretty strong to be fair.

"Did you not think to keep them once they were cut off?" the colour sergeant asked.

"No Colour."

"Did you get the medics to sign for them?"

"No Colour."

"Then you need to sign here so I can bill you for them." The CQMS passed a folder to Danny, pointed to the dotted line that said "Signature" and handed him a pen. "Sign there." he instructed.

Danny signed on the line, and the exact amount was deducted from his wages the following month under the description "Stores."

A bloke I knew in D Company broke his back while supervising army cadets rock-climbing and became paralysed from the chest down. Taff was a super-friendly corporal who everyone liked. He lived on the married quarters in Aldershot and whenever he came into a room in the accommodation block you'd hear him shout in his strong Welsh accent "Who's in ere then? Taff's in the basha!" We got the news that he'd broken his back and was being treated in Stoke Mandeville Hospital, so a load of us jumped in a minibus and went to pay him a visit. On the way we stopped to get him a card and searched through the selection to find one that wasn't too soppy in the "get well soon" section, but this proved difficult.

"How about this one?" one of the blokes suggested, offering a "good luck" card for us to look at. The picture on the front was of a man rock climbing, reaching at full stretch for his next handhold across a high void. The inspirational words "Reach for your goals" were also on the card.

"Yes! Perfect!" we said, and we bought it, taking it back to the minibus.

"Jesus Christ, we can't give him that! Who the fuck chose that?" The driver was older than the rest of us and had known Taff for years. "Screw the nut lads!" he said, he's fucking paralysed!"

We convinced him it was funny, and that Taff would like it, and we all signed it, but to be honest, I don't think he was all that impressed really, the poor bloke was in tatters and permanently disabled.

When you hear that someone has been in a motorbike accident, you assume that it was a high speed collision or crash. Several soldiers that I've known have suffered nasty injuries on motorbikes. One bloke was decapitated in a head-on collision, another lost a leg when he fell off and slammed into a post, and plenty of others have suffered broken bones, cuts, and bruises. My old friend Dale came off his motorbike going only fifteen miles per hour, as he negotiated a roundabout. A slippery, oil-spattered inspection cover on the ground caused him to fall during his turn, but his injuries were still significant. I was unable to visit Dale in hospital because of work commitments, but one of our mutual friends went to see him. Adam is a typical loud, boisterous, gobby northerner, who loves nothing more than verbally abusing his mates; the perfect guest when you're feeling sorry for yourself. At the time of Adams arrival Dale's mum was already there at his bedside, obviously upset and concerned for her son's wellbeing. As he got close, Adam noticed a colostomy bag hanging from the side of Dales bed after surgeons had operated on his aorta and his bowel. Dale hadn't even noticed him approaching when he bellowed.

"Fuck me Dale, you always were a bag of shit! And now you're two bags of shit!" Subtle as a brick! Adam himself was badly wounded some years later too. Hit by a roadside bomb in Iraq, while working as a security consultant, he seriously injured his leg, and almost ended up on his own colostomy bag after damaging his large intestine.

GRANDAD DIDN'T TALK ABOUT THE WAR

When I was a kid there were still loads of veterans from World War Two about, and most kids' grandparents had been involved in the conflict in one way or another. I remember hearing lots of adults say things like "He doesn't like to talk about it." Or "He never speaks about what he did in the war." when they talked about the former sailors, soldiers, or airmen in their families. I never met my grandfathers, so I never got to ask them, but as an ex-serviceman myself, I think I can relate to these stories of inhibition and reluctance to volunteer information. Don't get me wrong, I'm in no way comparing my operational experiences to what they may have endured in the bloodiest war the world has ever seen, I'm merely trying to empathise with the psychological and emotional side.

On return from Afghanistan in 2006 we were given some leave, and I'd been home for about a week when two good friends from the Pathfinders, Warren and Gaz came to my house. I made us all a brew, and we sat and talked for an hour or so, enjoying each other's company and having plenty of laughs. My son was only a few months old at the time, and I wanted to introduce him to them because they were close friends, and Warren was going to be his Godfather too. When they left I noticed my wife seemed to be acting a bit "off" with me.
"Everything alright?" I asked her.
"Yep." she replied, not looking at me as she walked past.
Clearly I'd done something to annoy her. "Obviously, it isn't al-

right." I said, and after a bit of persistence she explained why she was in a mood.

"Since you've been back, you haven't said a single thing to me about what you did over there, but your mates come round, and I suddenly hear more in an hour while you talk to them, than I've heard in a week!"

I imagine it was like that for the old boys from the Second World War, and every other conflict too. It's not necessarily that they don't want to talk about it, although some won't, it's probably more because they don't want to have to explain it to people who have no similar experiences. Soldiers speak their own language, and that includes being able to say things without actually saying them, omit parts of a story that may cause upset, and respectfully edit details to protect each other. They also know when it's appropriate to ask for more detail or question something stated as a fact. For example, many civilians think it's perfectly acceptable to ask a soldier if they've ever killed someone, but that's not something one soldier asks another because that is personal, that's his business not yours.

In the old days it must have been horrendous for the war veterans. PTSD wasn't really even a thing until the 1980's, and even then it took a long time to become recognised like it is today. I remember as a kid, people talking about veterans who'd got "shell shock" or "battle shock" and the way it was explained to me was that they'd been close to explosions that had sent them a bit crazy. Imagine spending months, if not years in trenches, being bombarded day-in, day-out, hearing about thousands of fellow soldiers dying in other fields of battle, while you knew nothing about the welfare of your family back home. Those young men suffered long periods of harsh brutality, facing, and surrounded by death every day, and no doubt hundreds of thousands of them suffered with undiagnosed PTSD. No wonder they didn't talk about it to their families. Why put anyone else through such torment? They suffered it so that others didn't have to.

ALL I WANTED WAS HAIR LIKE RAMBO

As a soldier there were only two things I wanted to accomplish beyond my military career. Completing 22 years would mean retiring at age 40 and for a while it seemed my long term aspirations were realistically achievable. The first was to grow my hair like John Rambo's in First Blood and First Blood 2. I'd had a shaven head since I was about sixteen and I thought that would be a good way to break out of the mould, to start anew. The second was to join the police. A few friends had done it, and it seemed the closest thing to being in the military; structured, honourable, and secure. I'd still be relatively young and fit and could begin a whole new career.

The Rambo haircut fantasy was scuppered when I realised I was going bald at about thirty years old. I don't know how most people discover they are losing their hair, maybe they get told by the barber or hairdresser, but I've always cut my own hair with a set of clippers, so nobody ever got that close to have a look. I found out in a Tesco superstore. I was standing in an entrance way, waiting for my wife to come out when I looked up at a black and white CCTV monitor on the wall. The camera showed the back of a man, who was holding a carrier bag in his right hand. I noticed he was going bald on top, at the back of his head. "I wonder if he knows that he's going bald?" I thought to myself. It looked like it had just started to go. The carrier bag was digging into my fingers, so I switched it to my left hand, and to my utter disappointment, so did the bloke on the CCTV a split second afterwards. I realised I was watching myself, and that's how I found out I was going bald. Gutted!

When my hearing deteriorated to the point where I was failing hearing tests a doctor asked me what I would do if I was discharged from the army because of it.

"I'd join the police." I answered. "That's my plan in a few years anyway, once I've done my twenty two years." I didn't think I'd get discharged, there were loads of blokes with bad hearing.

The doctor told me that she had worked with the police before. "You won't get in the police with hearing like yours." She said. "The police standard is much higher than the level you're at now."

I was gutted. "Really?" I asked. "Is it black and white like that, will I definitely not be allowed to join?"

"One hundred percent." She confirmed. "No way."

I hadn't realised how bad it was. "Would I be able to join the army with my hearing at this standard?" I queried.

"No, you wouldn't be allowed." She told me.

A few old mates used to cheat every time they had a hearing test. One bloke was quite deaf in one ear and used to swap the headphones round when the beeps changed sides, so he could use his good ear for both. Another mate used to just count to three and press the button every three seconds. One time he was sat there doing that with his eyes shut and felt a tap on the shoulder. It was the medic, stood in the open doorway looking at him forlornly. He removed the headset guiltily.

"It's finished!" she said disapprovingly.

He passed.

AN AIRBORNE TOAST

In 2014, when my time in the Pathfinders was coming to an end, I searched for a quote, or speech that I could use as part of my leaving presentation. I came across the airborne toast below, and it really resonated with me. To me it epitomises the ethos of the Airborne Brotherhood.

I have ridden the skies in great machines, I hooked up and jumped with the very best of men. I have fought long and hard, and when I felt I had no energy left, I have been fired by the fear that if I stopped fighting, my brothers would die. And when I was in danger, enemy all around, I heard the thunder from my left and my right, as my life was defended by these very same brothers. I have never been alone. For I lived, jumped, sweat, bled, cursed, drank, fought, and battled to victory with the greatest assemblage of men on earth.

Gentlemen, to the brotherhood of the airborne.

To the airborne! - *Jose N Harris, American Paratrooper.*

CHAPTER THREE

Jekyll and Clyde

WHATSHISNAME

In a battalion there are some very common names, and you could have several friends called, Smudge, Scotty, Taff, Jock, Paddy, Geordie, Scouse, Mac, H and Ginge. Sometimes they are differentiated by a prefix, and in the Parachute Regiment I had mates who were known as Scottish Smudge, Black Smudge, Big Scotty, Little Scotty, Taff B, Taff O'B, Geordie Simmo, Geordie Smudge, Scouse Smudge, Mad Mac, and Taff H. One of my mates called Ginge isn't even ginger, his hair is brown.

I phoned one of my best mates at home once and his mum answered.
"Hello, is Scotty there please?" I asked her.
Unexpectedly she replied, "Which one? There's three of them here."
I hadn't thought about it, but his dad and brother were also both in the army, and they were known as Scotty as well. At that point I realised that I didn't actually know my good friends name.
"The tall one." I answered, his dad was Para Reg too, and much shorter than my mate.
"Which one? There's two of them." She queried, clearly she'd done this before.
"Skinny....3 PARA....black hair." I blurted out.
"You mean Richard." She informed me, before calling him to the phone.
"Erm, yes?" I said.
Every day's a school day.

When I was in 3 PARA Signals Platoon we used to hang out with the Anti-tank Platoon a lot. One of the blokes in the "Tanks" was called Ben, but for about six months we called him Andy. We weren't trying to be funny, for some reason we really thought that was his name. One day, I was talking to another mate from the Tanks called Stu and asked him if Andy was going out that night.

"Andy who?" Stu replied.

"Tanks' Andy." I clarified. "Is he coming out?"

Stu looked stumped. "There isn't an Andy in the Tanks!"

Now I was stumped. "Eh? Yes there is, Geordie Andy! He was with us last night you lunatic!" I said.

"You mean Ben?" Stu offered. "Do you think Ben's name is Andy? Have you been calling him Andy all this time?" He was laughing now in disbelief. "His name is Ben you mad bastard!" he said.

The next time I saw Ben I asked him why he'd never said anything.

"I thought it was just a nickname." He answered. "I just went along with it."

From then on it was his nickname because we carried on calling him Andy anyway.

I knew how he felt because there was a bloke in 3 PARA who called me "Jonah" for years.

In my first platoon in A Company, 3 PARA there was a big bloke called Clyde who looked like a cross between a 70's porn star and a circus strongman. He had a big bushy moustache, a decent head of hair compared to most of us, and a hairy chest. He was a Private but looked about the same age as the Sergeant Majors. He'd been in Battalion quite a while and got pretty much left alone, working as the Company Armourer. One day I heard someone call him Clive and started to wonder if I'd got it wrong, then over the course of the day realised that some people definitely called him Clyde and some Clive. I asked one of the older soldiers which was correct.

"His name is Clyde." He said confidently, putting my mind at ease.

Later on I asked another bloke "Why do you call the Armourer Clive?"

He answered with equal authority. "Because that's him name! Why else would I call him it?"

That evening I went into Clyde's room. He was the only man in there, the other seven bedspaces were empty, apart from a few Pad's lockers. After a bit of small talk I asked him. "Is your name Clyde or Clive?"

"I don't really know Steve, whatever you prefer mate." He replied. "I don't mind."

I hate not knowing people's names, so I persisted. "But which is correct? I could have sworn it was Clyde."

"It's Clyde then." He said. "Stick with that."

I never did find out. I think it was neither to be honest, probably a nickname that had been given years before, and since lost its significance.

Other blokes I know, whose real names were a mystery to most of their friends:

Known as	Real Name	Reasoning
Terry	Stuart	Surname was Waite, and Terry Waite is a famous kidnap victim
Bosh	Stuart	Looked like another soldier called Si Hovey, hence; **B**rother **O**f **Si** **H**ovey
Prig	Mark	Said to resemble a dog in N.I called Prig
Ted	Paul	Surname was Danson, and Ted Danson is a famous actor from the T.V show "Cheers"
Beef	Jim	Surname was Stock, and beef stock sachets used to be in ration packs
Beef	Kirtin	Beef curtains is a crude nickname for ladyparts
Meathead	Dave	Bloke considered to have an oversized head
Worm	Ian	Surname Wornham
Moff	Tim	Surname Moffat
Peanut	Jason	Head shaped like a peanut
Dolly	Phil	Head like a porcelain doll's

Ronnie	Pete	Surname was O'Sullivan, and Ronnie O'Sullivan is a famous snooker player
Wang-eye	Matt	One of his eyes was off-centre
Chod	Alan	Rumoured to be well endowed
Tommy	Adam	Apparently Tommy Bennett was someone famous
Shafty	Jay	Said to look like 70's movie character John Shaft
Mac	Mark	Surname was McFadden
Jambo	Rohan	Said to look like a Kenyan boy. Jambo means "Hello" in Swahili
Freddie		Surname Kruyer, close enough to (Freddie) Kruger from Nightmare on Elm Street movies
Tommy	Colin	Surname was Tucker. Little Tommy Tucker is an old nursery rhyme
Billy	Michael	Surname Blanchard
Harry	Ian	Surname Harrison
Kebab	Mark	Surname Kibbard, close enough to kebab
Croc	Tim	Was from Australia
Emlyn	David	Surname Hughes, and Emlyn Hughes was a famous footballer
Camel	Kieran	Head like a camel
Ghost	Unknown	Unknown (Ironic)

SPLIT PERSONALITIES

The first ten weeks of my recruit training were done at Depot Para, Whittington Barracks, Lichfield. We formed up on 31 May 1993 and were the second ever platoon to begin training there after the closure of Depot Para, Browning Barracks in Aldershot, which had been the home of Parachute Regiment recruits since 1968. On our last day in Lichfield we were introduced to the staff from Catterick that would be taking us through the next sixteen weeks of training, and it became clear that we would be going through the whole process of dehumanisation and proving ourselves worthy once again.

"You fuckers have had it easy down here in this little holiday camp!" our new Platoon Sergeant shouted at us. "You lot don't know what a beasting is yet, but you'll soon find out once we start smashing you in Catterick!" It seemed a bit disrespectful to our current instructors to suggest they'd gone easy on us, but I guess it was part of the plan. He wanted us to know how much harder the training was about to get once he got his hands on us and made a point of telling us how the recruits who were already there were dropping like flies. "We've got twenty-two fractures in one single platoon up there!" he boasted. "Fucking brace yourselves boys, you are mine now!" We already understood the hierarchical structure after ten weeks of intense graft, but they were intent on re-establishing our worthlessness as mere Crows who were there to be beasted and to clarify their status as gods whose word was law. In the last few frantic moments before we departed on summer leave I was sent on a task to return some equipment to the stores, and while I was gone the rest of the platoon were called into the corridor to be briefed on a change of information. Unbeknown to me, they were told that the original date we had been given to start in Catterick was incorrect, and they amended it to a day earlier. In a time before everyone had mobile phones, I never received that rather important piece of information and based my plans on the old, superseded date.

The day I walked through the gate of Helles Barracks in Catterick Garrison, North Yorkshire the man in the guardroom seemed surprised to see me.

"I thought you Para recruits all turned up yesterday!" he stated.

My heart sank. "What?!" I said, wide eyed and immediately filled with dread.

He turned towards another man in the guardroom and called out.

"The Para lot all came in yesterday didn't they Alan?"

"Yep. They had to be here before two o'clock yesterday." He replied.

The first man looked back towards me. "I reckon you're late young man!"

"You're fucking kidding me!" I said glumly, this was the worst possible way to start!

Within a couple of minutes a Parachute Regiment corporal collected me and silently led me to the accommodation block, where I dropped my bags and marched to the staff office door, halting smartly, and standing to attention. Sat behind a desk was my new Platoon Sergeant, who looked at me with contempt, like he already hated me.

Nervously, I introduced myself. "Sergeant, I am Private Brown, reporting for duty. I think I might be late Sergeant."

"You fucking dough-ball Brown, you're fucking right you're late! A whole day late!" he said sternly in a strong Scottish accent.

I'd never been called a dough-ball before, but I was pretty sure it wasn't a compliment. Arriving late ensured that I got last dibs on the bed spaces, and my new sergeant showed me to it. It was the closest bed to the platoon office, which meant I'd always be one of the first to get stiffed with all the crappy jobs the instruct-

STEVE BROWN

ors wanted doing. Missing a parade, or being late was a chargeable offence, and a few days later I reported to the Headquarters building, to receive my punishment from the Major who was Officer Commanding Recruit Company.

One of the many infamous people in the Parachute Regiment during my time was a man called Dave Pete, who was often referred to as "Dave and Pete" because of his seemingly split personality. Like Jekyll and Hyde it was somewhat of a gamble who you would find yourself talking to on any given encounter. My first and only interaction with him was in Depot Para, while I was waiting to be charged by the O.C.

Dave was a Colour Sergeant and would be marching me in to the office. He briefly explained how the procedure would work, and presented me with a large, heavy, red book titled The Queen's Regulations for The Army.

"Read that." He said, handing me the huge document. "That tells you all about your rights and what to expect when the O.C charges you."

I opened the red leather front page and turned a few pages slowly in a token gesture. Obviously, I wasn't expected to actually read it, that would take hours, if not days. Ten minutes later Dave returned.

"Have you read the Queen's Regs?" he asked.

Clearly lying, but playing the game I answered, "Yes Colour, I have."

He acted surprised. "You've read all that, already?" he questioned, pointing at the book.

"I've skimmed through it Colour, yes." I said.

Dave spoke sincerely and gave me some advice. "Brown, you need to read through that document properly to you give yourself the best chance of a good outcome. Take your time, absorb the information and let me know when you are finished, there's a good lad." he said, before he disappeared down the corridor once more. He seemed like a nice bloke, and much more approachable than the other staff. A short time later he returned to check my progress again.

"Finished?" he asked.

I was grateful for the advice but didn't know where to start with the book and had read about ten words of a random page. "Finished Colour, yes." I bluffed.

He snatched the book away from me. "Well that was a fucking waste of time! Because you're guilty as charged anyway you little shit! You've got no rights! You were fucking late, and you'll get what's coming to you! Do you understand me Brown?!"

"Yes Colour!" I replied, a little startled, and confused.

I'd just met Pete!

I received five days of restricted privileges, or RP's as my punishment and marched immediately to the guardroom to present myself to the Provost Staff, who are like the local enforcers on camp. The Provost Corporal was a huge Parachute Regiment lance corporal who had been expecting me. I was stood to attention in his office when he stopped right in front of me, looking down at me angrily.

"RP's. RP's… shun!" he shouted. The command for me to come to attention.

Already at attention I stood still, which was the right thing to do, but seemingly he wasn't up to speed with drill himself.

"Switch on Brown you fucking retard! We'll try that again shall we?" he screamed in my face before giving me the incorrect order again. "RP's…..Shun!"

Sure that I was doing the right thing, I again stood still, with my arms pinned to my sides and heels together, chin up high. This was awkward.

"You are pissing me off Brown! You better start paying fucking attention, or your five days will be turning into ten and I will beast you to death! Do you understand me?" He was livid, and clearly hadn't noticed I was already at attention.

"Yes Corporal!" I replied. Whatever I did was wrong, but only one of us knew that, and the next time he gave the command I simply raised my leg and slammed my foot back into the same position.

"At last! You really are stupid aren't you Brown!" he said ironically. One of us was definitely more stupid than the other.

As if Depot wasn't hard and hectic enough, I now had to parade for inspection at the guardroom at 0600hrs, 1230hrs and 2200hrs as well as 1600hrs for a two-hour work detail of sweeping leaves or polishing brass. It was hideous.

THE BOULTON TWINS

A great soldier who looked out for me as a new bloke was my good friend Steve Boulton. He was a lance corporal in my first platoon in A Company, 3 Para and was always there to help the new guys out. His attitude taught me the difference in outcomes when people work for someone out of respect for rank, versus respect for the person. We'd always voluntarily graft for him and gladly go the extra mile, compared to a few other corporals who we'd work for resentfully because they acted like pricks. I'd known Steve for a good few months when an old friend of his asked me if I'd met his twin brother yet. Nathan had known him for years, and they'd served in B Company together before Steve was promoted and moved to A Company. I knew he had younger brothers, but he'd never mentioned a twin.

One weekend Steve came to stay at my old house in Aylesbury for a night out and we went into town with my oldest friend Mayur for beers. Before long we were getting well-oiled, and Steve was taking lead vocals for some airborne songs with Mayur, a fully-fledged civilian reluctantly joining in at Steve's insistence. At about 2230hrs we caught a taxi to a nightclub a few miles out of town and after queuing up outside for a while, continued drinking in there. After an hour or so and a few more beers, Steve asked me to hold his drink while he disappeared to the toilet, and a couple of minutes later he returned, or at least someone who looked like him returned. Before I saw him, my attention was drawn by another man falling over backwards, arms flailing, as he tried to keep his balance. A second man quickly followed suit but managed to stay on his feet, and all eyes turned towards the man who was pushing and shoving his way through the mass of people.

Steve appeared through a gap in the crowd as everyone got out of his way and made his way towards me and Mayur. He looked different, his eyes were sunken and dark, and his face seemed to be drooping. Everyone he looked at got either pushed, slapped, or verbally abused and I could see groups of blokes looking across to us, planning a counter attack. We were by far, the least popular people in that bar, and without doubt heading for a massive kicking from all directions. Luckily, I knew the doormen and one of them was ex-army himself. I lied and told him Steve was just back from Northern Ireland and had had a rough time over there. Somehow, we got out in one piece, and that night I realised who Steve's twin brother was; drunk Steve, and drunk Steve was a very angry, aggressive, and volatile man. I met his twin a few times after that, each time involved alcohol and bloodshed.

Steve also suffered with a mild form of road rage. On a few occasions as he was the only one with a car, a white Vauxhall Montego, he drove us to the cinema in Bracknell. One day we were driving around the cinema car park, struggling to find a space when one of the blokes in the back spotted one. It was a one-way system, and nobody was in front of us, so it was ours. Steve was driving, I was in the passenger seat, and three other blokes were in the back. As we got close to the space a car turned into the lane from the opposite end and darted into our spot quickly, stealing it at the last minute with an illegal manoeuvre. A bloke was driving, but a pretty young woman jumped out of the passenger seat and waved at us apologetically as we drove past, so we let it go. We found another space easily enough and debussed, heading for the cinema. Following Steve as he walked briskly, weaving between the parked cars we stopped suddenly, Steve had navigated straight to the car in our rightful space. He pointed at the four of us individually as he spoke. "Front right! Front left! Back left! Back right! Go!"

Further instructions were not required, and we dutifully sprinted to our designated targets like a Formula One pit stop team, simultaneously letting down all four tyres of that car, laughing like little kids as we did it. It was very immature, but very funny. Small things amuse small minds.

Another day, in that same car park, we returned from the cinema to find a car on our right-hand side parked extremely close. Steve was snapping because he couldn't open the driver's door and had to climb across from the passenger side to get in. As I got in I heard him giggling and looked across to see that he'd wound down his window and was using a key to scratch the word "**KNOB**" in big, untidy letters into the paintwork of the offending car. That was also very immature, and only made funny by the crazed expression and manic laughter coming from Steve as he taught someone not to park like a knob.

SPIDER MAN AND MR. DUVAL

One Saturday morning, after a heavy night in Dover town, I bumped into one of the blokes called Adam in the accommodation corridor. I was walking out of the ablutions, and he was walking out of one of the six-man rooms, shaking his head. He looked up at me.

"Have you been in there?" he asked, pointing over his shoulder with his thumb to the room he'd exited.

"No, why?" I replied.

"You need to see it mate." Adam said.

I had a hangover and just wanted to go back to bed. "I'll look later." I told him.

Adam persisted, "You need to see what that mad bastard has done in there mate."

Intrigued, I went inside. Eight hundred feet of climbing rope was strung across that room, criss-crossing from every locker, bed, window, and table in a massive entanglement, it must have taken all night to produce. I ducked, crawled, and straddled over the rope to get to the bedspace of the occupant, a climbing enthusiast called Mike. He was fast asleep in his standard issue, single bed, still fully clothed from the previous night. On the floor next to his bed was a small tin of red paint with a brush sticking out from the top. Disturbingly, Mike had painted a red line across the throat of every single person in his bedspace, making it look like their throats had been slashed. Like most of the blokes, his walls and lockers were covered in pictures, mostly cut out from magazines but that was the first time I'd seen this sinister addition. He was an eccentric bloke, and at the time I thought it was more funny than strange. I woke him up and in his still-drunk state he explained the rope.

"Those fucking pads come in here every day and wake me up!" he said angrily. "I thought if I made a web, I could catch them, and they'd get stuck!"

"Pads" was the name given to married soldiers who lived on the married quarters, or "pads estate." Usually they would have a locker in the accommodation for their day to day kit, and unfortunately for Mike, his room was also the "pads locker" room.

On a separate night, Mike had been halted at the camp gate by a corporal called Tiddy who caught him walking out in his climbing kit. Tiddy was on guard duty and saw him staggering drunk through camp at about 0200hrs, wearing boots and carrying ice axes and crampons. Mike told him he was going to climb the white cliffs of Dover, but Tiddy denied him exit, and sent him back to the block for his own safety. Frustrated that he couldn't go climbing, Mike instead set up a small abseil from his first-floor bedroom, and was found asleep, dangling off the ground in his climbing harness in a contorted position later that morning.

In the Parachute Regiment adventure training was a kind of myth. You heard stories about it, saw recruitment pictures and videos advertising it, but never actually got to do it or met anyone else who'd done it. Seemingly it was reserved for the R.A.F and the non-ferocious regiments of the army. To my surprise, about four years into my time at 3 PARA we were all asked to choose the adventure training we wanted to do that year. A new officer had taken charge of our platoon and he still believed in things like Father Christmas, the Easter Bunny and Adventure Training. Not really believing it would happen anyway, I paid little attention to what was on offer and instead just made it clear there were only two things I did not want to do; climbing and caving.

My week-long pot-holing course, a mixture of climbing and caving, was held in North Yorkshire that winter, and the only other soldier to get put on it was Mike, who at the time, I hardly knew. What I did know, was that he was a climbing fanatic and a bit of an eccentric. I was absolutely dreading it! As it turned out we had a great time, not because of the activity, but because Mike was completely nuts and kept me laughing with his craziness throughout the week. Like me at the time, he detested everyone that wasn't Parachute Regiment and was also disproportionately aggravated by everything they said and everything they did. We were young and fit, but most of the other course attendees were middle aged submariners, that had a serious lack of social skills, and a lot less energy than us. At the end of that first day of crawling through dark, wet tunnels, and being constantly dripped on while you squeezed between jagged rocks, Mike and I decided we deserved a pint. The course was run from a small camp in Ripon, next to the Yorkshire Dales and we headed into town as soon as we got back, not inviting anyone else to come along.

Being typical Para Reg we scrutinised the soldier on the gate as we exited the barracks, angered by his lack of professionalism. Firstly, as we approached we noticed he had a radio playing music loudly. We looked at each other in disgust, the background noise would obviously compromise his ability to hear suspicious activity. As we got closer we saw him sat down inside the small sentry post, another no-no in our regiment, we didn't even have chairs on guard duty, that would compromise his response time. But the icing on the cake, the pièce de résistance was seeing his rifle leaning against the wall outside the sentry post; that compromised the security of the whole camp. Seething, we walked on and went into Ripon to get drunk.

Returning a few hours later a different soldier was now at the front gate, and as we approached he walked towards us. This guy hadn't gone as far as the last one with his slack drills, but he wasn't too far behind, and sauntered over with his rifle slung behind his back. "I.D please gents." He requested.

Mike, now full of beer, was unable to contain himself and started shouting in a voice that resembled Rik Mayall in The Young Ones. "Why is your weapon behind your back!?" He yelled. "How ready are you for a fucking terrorist attack!?"

The shocked soldier had no idea how to react. Mike sounded quite posh, but wasn't dressed like an officer, so he half stood to attention and began answering.

"Not very ready Sir!" he answered, "Can I.."

Before he could finish, Mike reached behind his own back with his right hand as if to grab something and pretended to pull a gun from his waistband, pointing his index and middle fingers in the blokes face like a pistol.

"Bang!" he shouted. "You'd be fucking dead wouldn't you!"

The soldier was obviously shocked but stood his ground. "Can I see some I.D please Sir?" he persisted.

Mike walked straight past him. "Don't speak to me you fucking creature!" he screamed angrily, entering camp unlawfully.

"Can I ask your name then please Sir?" he shouted after Mike.

"I'm Mr. DuVal!" came the random reply as he disappeared into the shadows of some trees.

I was drunk too, but I knew this was out of order. Very funny though. I showed my I.D and vouched for Mike. "It's alright, he's with me." I explained.

The following morning we paraded with the rest of the course to receive our daily weather update and training brief, but instead were told about an incident that had happened on the gate during the night. Unless the culprits owned up, there was going to be an identity parade with the soldier who'd been on duty. Mike put his hand up straight away.

"It was me." He confessed.

"It was me as well." I said, raising my hand too.

It was obviously the two Para Reg blokes, nobody was surprised, and we were sent directly to see the Regimental Sergeant Major of the camp. In our Battalion, getting sent to the RSM's office would have been a scary experience with a high likelihood of receiving a good old fashioned bollocking. Depending on their mood you'd expect a chest prodding at the very least, at worst you'd be getting knocked out. This man wasn't Para Reg though, and we were, and we were still drunk. We stood there arrogantly, looking at him with total disdain as he tried to be intimidating. He pointed at me first. "Name?"

"Private Brown Sir." I replied.

"Name?" he repeated, this time pointing at Mike.

"Private Ashton Sir." He answered.

The RSM looked at his notepad, then looked back up blankly. "So who the fuck is this DuVal character?"

Mike responded immediately. "I am Sir."

"I thought you said you were Ashton?" the RSM queried, clearly puzzled.

"That's correct Sir, I am." Mike stated firmly, adding to the confusion.

I was supposed to be worried, but instead I was doing my best not to laugh. I couldn't tell if he was doing it deliberately or just completely oblivious to the absurdity of the conversation, either way he was keeping the RSM off my back, so I didn't care.

"He's Brown, you're Ashton." The RSM confirmed, with us nodding in agreement. "So who the fuck is DuVal?"

"I'm Ashton and DuVal Sir!" Mike blurted out.

The RSM shook his head and moved on with his reprimand, starting with a scene setter. "Lads, we've all been on guard duty before, none of us like it, but we have to do it because it's part of the job, and vital to security."

He wasn't wrong, guard duty was the bane of every Private soldier's life.

"Now, what's the worst thing about being stuck on the gate at night, when pissed-up idiots are coming back from a night down town?"

It was a loaded and leading question, and the obvious answer was "Drunk people acting like idiots while I'm just trying to do my job sir." But Mike beat me to it with his own response.

"People not holding their weapons correctly Sir!" he barked, somehow missing the cues, and answering from a completely different perspective.

The RSM shook his head. "No. No. Listen lads, what I'm saying is, when you're on guard and people start coming in acting lary..."

I felt like an interpreter. I knew exactly what they both meant.

"Drunk people gobbing off Sir." I said firmly.

We took a slap on the wrist and cracked on with the course. I still hate caving and climbing.

SOMEONE'S WATCHED TOO MUCH T.V

An old friend of mine in 3 PARA was called Pete Brunton. He joined battalion shortly after me, but unfortunately he never really settled down or fit in that well. Many of the blokes found him a bit strange, and kept it at arms distance, but I always gave him the benefit of the doubt, to me he just seemed a bit of an eccentric. He proved them right beyond reasonable doubt in the end though, because he transferred to the Royal Military Police, or as they're known in the army "The Monkeys." One day Pete reported sick at the Medical Centre after injuring an ankle during P.T. It was fair enough, he was in a lot of pain, and it was swollen, anyone with an ounce of common sense would have done exactly the same to make sure it wasn't broken or dislocated. Not being particularly popular though, he was quickly labelled a bluffer by a few of the others when he returned with a sick note that gave him seven days "light duties." The doctor prescribed him the army's standard medical treatment package of Tubigrip and Brufen (Ibuprofen) and told him to avoid running but try swimming instead. Rather unjustified, by pretty funny, from then on his nickname was Pete Brufen. Pete used to like covering his face in camouflage cream and jumping out on people when they returned from a night out. He did it to me once as I walked into my room in Aldershot. It was an eight-man room, so when I entered I didn't turn the light on in case anyone else was sleeping. When Pete suddenly appeared beside me from the darkness, his face just visible from the light cast through the porous issue curtains, I instinctively kicked him with a side-kick to the stomach, sending him sprawling backwards across the room. He was quite upset about that, protesting that it was only a joke and there was no need to hit him, but I told him it was a stupid thing to do and to piss off somewhere else. Intent on spooking someone he stayed in my room, and I saw him crawl under the bed of another soldier who was yet to return from town.

The next day I bumped into him while walking through camp and noticed he still had a small spot of green camouflage cream in his ear, where he'd failed to wash it all off.

"What the fuck were you doing last night you silly twat?" I said scathingly. "Creeping around the block in cam cream like a sex-case!"

Pete answered me in a quiet, husky tone. "I was adapting, improvising, and overcoming. Got to prepare for combat, expect the unexpected!"

Strangely, he was also speaking with an American accent, and sounded like someone on the other end of a "heavy-breather" nuisance call.

I was puzzled. He seemed serious, with no hint of humour. "Why are you talking like that?" I said.

Pete glanced around nervously, quickly scanning the surroundings before looking back into my eyes. "Talking like what?" he replied, in the same tone.

"Like a fucking American with a sore throat!" I told him.

His answer was delivered straight faced and sincerely, like it was a perfectly acceptable explanation for his weird behaviour.

"I watched Heartbreak Ridge three times yesterday." He said. "Now I talk like this."

I looked at him for a couple of seconds, taking it all in. Heartbreak Ridge is a film about the U.S Marine Corps, starring Clint Eastwood, and in that film he talks quietly with a thick rasp to his tone. I nodded my head slightly several times in resignation. Now was not the time for sensible conversation or reasoning.

"Okay mate." I said. "See you later."

I don't know how long he kept that up for, but the next time I saw him he was back to his own version of normal.

TRAUMA HORMER

Every day in battalion the privates conduct area cleaning under the supervision of the duty corporal. If you hadn't got up for breakfast, it was likely the first thing you'd hear in the morning was the corporal walking through the corridor shouting "outside for area cleaning!"

One morning I was woken by the familiar voice of John B, giving the call from outside the building.

In his strong brummie accent he was shouting. "Everyone outside now!" He was a good friend of mine and I could tell he sounded angry. I opened my first floor window to see him standing on the ground below with a handful of blokes.

"Come on Ste, get down here, and bring all the other silly fuckers with you!" he said.

"What's the matter mate?" I asked him. He was obviously very agitated.

John B pointed to the wall below my room. "Do you know what knob-head did this?" he quizzed.

I couldn't see the wall from my position and looked at him blankly. "No idea mate." I replied.

"Come down here Ste" he repeated. "We need to sort this out."

Gathering the other three blokes in my room we walked down the stairs and outside to where John B was stood. Word had got round that he was pissed off, so everyone had come outside, not wanting to get on the wrong side of the well-respected soldier. Painted on the wall, in bold green letters, two feet tall, were the words "**O.C D IS PRICK!**" We were in D Company, and our Officer Commanding was a major who had apparently been a bare-knuckle boxer in his youth and compared to a lot of the others was reasonably well liked. We started laughing but John B stopped us. "This ain't fucking funny lads, the O.C is gonna go mental!"

It was funny. The grammar was terrible, the handwriting was a mess, and it was obviously written by someone very drunk. We all knew that Recce Platoon had been out drinking the previous night, and there were two likely suspects on everyone's mind straight away, but we kept quiet. Trauma Hormer and Dom H were both absent from area cleaning, they both disliked the O.C, and they were both mental after a few pints. It was bound to be one of them. Adding suspicion on the Recce Platoon was the fact that they had been re-painting their equipment with the Company recognition colour the day before, and D Company's colour was green. John B sent us off to litter-pick and sweep the leaves in our designated area and stayed behind to conduct an investigation. Unsupervised, we briskly walked the route, pretending not to see any rubbish or cigarette ends and quickly returned to the block. John B's police work was already complete by the time we got back, and he was already halfway through an interrogation when I entered the room of my friend James "Trauma" Hormer.

As far as I know John B had not attended the Tracking Instructors course but seeing as though Trauma had most definitely not attended a Counter-Tracking course, he'd managed to interpret the ground sign, and followed the evidence directly to Trauma's bedspace. Drips of paint led from the crime scene outside, through the entrance way, along the corridor, into a ground-floor room, to a closed locker. On opening the locker John B found a tin of green paint and a brush with paint on the handle. In bed next to said locker was Trauma, still sleeping off the alcohol he'd consumed, with green paint all over his hands. After an initial plea of innocence, Trauma conceded it was him and braced himself for a disciplinary interview with the O.C.

Apparently when the Major asked him why he'd done it, he nonchalantly replied. "It's just the way you come across Sir!"

Cementing his infamy amongst the blokes, Trauma once joined a group of 3 PARA soldiers who went into Dover town centre to avenge one of the men, who'd been attacked by a gang of civilians in a pub. This was not an unusual response, more of a standard operating procedure if one of our own was unjustifiably assaulted. Normally it would be initiated by the guard commander back in camp, who, on hearing the news, would deploy his men to the accommodation blocks to rally the other paratroopers. The blokes would eagerly cram themselves into cars like the Anthill Mob and drive quickly into town to mete out punishment. On this occasion Trauma was sent into the pub first to get a reaction from the offenders before the others followed, the logic being that if they all went in at once the offenders would keep quiet and be difficult to identify. Trauma was a relatively small bloke, but walked in like a king gorilla, watched from the outside by the others. Seeing a group of men sat at the bar he stood facing them, proudly wearing his maroon, Parachute Regiment t-shirt.

"Are you the fucking pricks that had a go at my mate?" he said boldly.

One of the men looked at him and responded dismissively. "Fuck off, or you'll get the same!"

Taking that as an admission of guilt, Trauma immediately picked up a barstool and launched it at the arrogant bully, who ducked instinctively as it flew over his head, across the bar, and into the bottles of upturned spirits behind the counter. As the bottles smashed, the remainder of the blokes ran into the pub, resulting in a bar brawl with a predictable outcome. Just like you wouldn't walk into a Hell's Angels bar and pick a fight with a biker, it's not a good idea to attack soldiers in their adoptive home towns either.

THE JEDI

When the Company Sergeant Major is coming to the end of his tenure in charge, the soldiers start investigating who his replacement might be. Depending on who they have at the time they might be grateful for anyone else, or sad to see them go. When I was in D Company, 3 PARA, we heard rumours that our incoming sergeant major was a man called Jed Williams. He was a well-known, long serving member of 1 PARA, known as The Jedi, and the stories about him came in thick and fast, mostly about insane feats of physical performance. I don't know if they were true, but I remember being told that he'd do ten mile speed marches carrying jerry cans of water, beat everyone on two mile fitness tests carrying a machine gun instead of a rifle, and complete all the airborne fitness tests back to back in one go, rather than over a period of weeks. One of my mates was working in the sergeants mess and was telling us how he'd seen him talking to his food, threatening it. He said he was separating the different ingredients on his plate, making small piles of each, and heard him say.
"Ah, peas. I'm gonna fucking eat you last!"
We needn't have worried though, he was awesome, a bits nuts, but awesome.

A friend of mine spent three months with him in Norway and said he didn't use a tent once during the whole trip. We'd work from a base camp in Norway but spend a lot of time in the field on exercise, usually sleeping in ten-man, five-man, or four-man tents to protect us from the harsh winter climate. Not Jedi, he'd build igloos, snow caves and trenches, or just sleep outside under the stars. He was old school, hardcore.

One night The Jedi decided we should have some fun and organised a bobsleigh race down a large hill close to where we were camped. As instructed, we paraded at the top of the hill with our pulks, which we'd emptied of all the equipment they carried. The pulks were sleds that were normally used to carry heavy equipment like tents, rations, and ammunition but that night they would be improvised bobsleighs. Jedi welcomed us and briefed us on the activity. Placed down the slope clipped onto ski poles dug into the ground were several glow-sticks which represented a slalom course. On Jedis command teams of four men were to negotiate the course as quickly as possible, the fastest team winning, subject to penalty points for missing a pole. He explained the best configuration was three men facing forwards and the rear man facing rearwards. The rear man's job was to steer by digging in his heels on either side, and the remainder would assist him by leaning. It sounded simple enough. The first team got ready, closely watched by the rest of us so we could learn from their mistakes. Sprinting to the start line, two men on either side pushing the pulk they looked quite well organised, as they jumped onto it on the line, and held on to each other tightly. Despite them all shouting commands to go left towards the first pole and the rear man trying his best to steer, they shot straight down the hill, missing the first, then second, then every other pole as they hurtled down that slope at a rapid rate of knots, completely out of control and at the mercy of gravity. It was a pathetic attempt at slalom but an impressive crack at breaking the over-snow land speed record. We all laughed at them, convinced we'd fare much better, but the same thing happened to every single team, with some crashing spectacularly and others disappearing into the darkness, unable to stop. Somehow nobody got injured and we had a good night entertaining The Jedi.

MY MATES ARE PROBABLY HARDER THAN YOUR MATES

The Parachute Regiment is full of hard nuts. Not just people who profess to be hard because everyone in their insignificant little home town tells them they are. I mean real hard nuts, blokes from your darkest fucking nightmares, prepared to do things that would make the average man sick. As a young man I had a reputation for being quite handy, but I can honestly say that there were blokes in Para Reg that I would have gladly crawled over broken glass covered in pig shit, to avoid getting into a fight with when I joined 3 PARA. I liken infantry battalions to prisons, or gangs, or anywhere that has a predominantly male population with a high potential for aggression and violence. Each will have its tough guys, fighters, alpha males, psychopaths, psychotics, and sociopaths, but in my opinion, the Parachute Regiment will have more than its fair share.

Some of the stories I've heard about Para Reg blokes are like some kind of folklore or urban legend, maybe they're true, maybe they're not. Most likely they are somewhere in the middle, with details omitted or added over time to make the story more palatable to the audience. One of the people I heard the most stories about was "Scouse" who's mere name being mentioned will evoke a response from the thousands of blokes that have met or heard about him. Apparently he was challenged a few times by people who wanted to test themselves or prove themselves by fighting a man with such a status. I was told that one man attacked him unprovoked with a powerful head butt to the face. Scouse recoiled with the force, then, with blood running from his nose calmly responded.

"I'm only going to hit you once, but I'm going to hit you very, very hard!" He hit that bloke with such power, it broke his jaw, knocked him unconscious and he spent the night in hospital after an ambulance was called. The story goes that the following week, the same man approached Scouse in the same bar and passed him a pint of beer.

"No hard feelings mate. I'm getting out of the army and thought I'd see for myself if you were as nails as everyone says you are, and fair play, you are." He explained.

They shook hands, and the legend continued.

In 3 PARA there was a big Cornish bloke called Kev, who I saw knock out three grown men in succession like they were children. I was leaving a nightclub in Aldershot called "Limelight's" when there was a scuffle and a load of shouting in the street outside the main entrance. A gang of civilians were on the other side of the road shouting angrily, and one of them walked towards Kev.

"We're the Birmingham Boys!" he yelled. "What you gonna fucking do about it!?"

Without even adjusting his stance, Kev punched the bloke with a lightning fast right hand and dropped him to the tarmac unconscious.

A second man stepped forward. "You can't do that, we're the fucking Birmingham Boys!" he screamed. He too was knocked out the second he got within Kev's range, and lay on the road next to his sleeping friend. The women in the group were screaming hysterically, and a third man made an ill-advised attempt to avenge the honour of the infamous Birmingham Boys, rushing towards Kev. He fared no better. Three men knocked out in three punches was impressive to watch. The police were on scene very quickly, obviously loitering nearby, anticipating trouble, and everyone left, well everyone who was awake anyway.

In 2 PARA there was a bloke with such a fearsome reputation that when he attended courses, the instructors would actively try to ensure he wasn't put in their team. Infantry courses are normally quite harsh, with students regularly receiving verbal and physical beastings for misdemeanours and trivial mistakes, but the prospect of having to reprimand this soldier terrified them. On one course he approached his instructor, put an arm around his shoulders and hugged him tight.

"How did I get on?" he asked. "Distinction, yes!?"

The instructor affirmed his prediction at achieving an outstanding grade.

"Distinction? Yes, I think so." He replied, nodding nervously.

The strange thing about that conversation was that it happened on day one of the twelve week course, before lessons had even started. He was right as well, he did get a distinction.

JOE DABROWSKI

My best friend in 3 PARA for several years was Joe Dabrowski. Joe was a very fit, 6'2", 14 stone heavyweight boxer from the Midlands, whose personality depended on what was going on in his personal life. By default, he was an extremely well mannered, slightly old-fashioned, kind, and generous young man. However, when people upset him, his friends, or God forbid, his family, there was another side to him that could manifest itself, with a huge, unpredictable potential for anger and violence, a bit like the 1980's, Lou Ferrigno version of The Incredible Hulk. In a moment of terrible judgement, some idiot decided that Joe should be posted to the Officers Mess, to see out the last six months of his career. Three of those months were in Norway, where we would deploy as a battalion to conduct arctic warfare training. Every now and then I'd pass through the camp where Joe was stationed and seek him out for a catch-up. He was pretty angry back then. He'd split up with his girlfriend because he was always away, he'd been refused early release and subsequently lost an excellent job opportunity, and now he was working in the mess, clearing up after irritating young officers. One day in the mess, an R.A.F officer wanted Joe's attention and summoned him arrogantly.

"Waiter." he called out.

Joe paused momentarily, thinking he'd heard someone call out "waiter" but dismissing it immediately. Nobody would be that condescending.

"Waiter." came the call a second time.

Joe turned around to see the officer sat at his table looking towards him expectantly and walked towards him, barely containing himself. Approaching from the side, Joe bent down to address him, placing a hand on his shoulder, and squeezing his trapezius muscle tightly in a Vulcan death grip. Speaking into his ear in a sinister snarl he told him. "Sir, my name is not fucking Waiter, it's Private Dabrowski! If you want to speak to me you call me Private Dabrowski, or Joe, not fucking Waiter! Do you understand me?"

The startled officer apologised sincerely. "Yes Joe. Sorry Joe."

Another time he was making friends in the mess was during breakfast, when two officers turned up late. He watched one of them fill a bowl with cereal, then as he walked across to get some milk Joe picked up the ladle and serving bowl and walked off with it.

"Excuse me Joe, I need some milk please." He called.

Joe stopped and turned around. "Sir, what time does breakfast finish?" he asked abruptly.

"Six-thirty." The officer replied.

Joe continued. "And what time is it now?"

"Six-thirty-five." He conceded.

"Exactly. So you are late!" Joe snapped. "I've been up since five o'clock to make sure you can get your breakfast on time. Why should I get up at five if you can't be bothered to get up before half past six?" With that he walked off towards the kitchen, taking the milk with him.

The officer tried one last time. "Can I have some milk please?"

"Nope!" Joe called over his shoulder, as he walked off.

One Sunday, after returning from Christmas leave, Joe was telling me about a fight he'd gotten into at home in Shrewsbury. This was before the Norway exercise and right after the break-up with his girlfriend. Walking home after a night in town, his fast pace ensured he overtook anyone else heading in the same direction. As he brushed past one man he triggered an unexpected response.

"Watch where you're going, or I'll knock you the fuck out!" the stranger said threateningly.

Without turning around Joe replied. "Don't fucking bother mate!" he warned.

The man reached out, grabbing him by the arm aggressively, and Joe immediately turned on the spot, took his own grip, and pulled him towards him as he launched a devastating right hand to the chin. Joe described to me how he hit him again as he fell and then went to kneel on his chest, but accidentally knelt on his face in his drunken state before correcting himself. Once in position he began punching the man in the head but then blanked out, and the next memory he had was kneeling on the man's chest looking down at his bloodied face and unconscious body.

I was laughing as he told me this, partly because I loved the violence of it, and partly out of shock, I'd never heard of someone blacking out in anger before.

"What did you do then?" I chuckled, excited to hear the next part of the psychotic story.

Joe explained how, like a good Samaritan, he placed the unconscious casualty in the ¾ prone recovery position and went home to bed.

To me that was the most outrageous part. "You fucking idiot, you might have killed him!" I laughed. Getting punched in the head by him an undetermined amount of times was not good for your health, you didn't have to be a brain surgeon to work that one out. Joe had obviously recognised this too, and diligently conducted his own thorough investigation into the man's medical status.

"I'm pretty sure he's not dead." he said unconvincingly. "I've been watching the news, and checked the local newspaper, and there was nothing about it on them. If he were dead, it would be all over the news!"

"Well there you go mate, he's fine, case closed." I said sarcastically.

Another idiot from Shrewsbury started on him once. Close to where he lived there were some local shops, and at the time there were a gang of young men who hung around outside them, regularly drawing complaints to the police for anti-social and abusive behaviour from customers. Joe found himself on the receiving end of the abuse one night because he'd taken the short walk to the shop wearing the shorts and flip flops he usually reserved for lounging around at home. As it was a cold winter night, this drew the unwanted attention of the troublemakers who noticed his attire as he left the shop with a six-pack of beers.

"Nice shorts!" said one.

"Yeah, I like your flip flops mate!" called another cockily.

Joe kept his cool, until a third comment came his way by a young man walking towards him.

"What the fuck do you think you're wearing?" he said rhetorically.

Joe was barely keeping a lid on it. "Go away, before you get hurt!" he warned.

The thug stood directly in Joe's path. "Really? What are you gonna do you wanker!?"

With that Joe slapped him round the side of the head hard, and the teenage gobshite slammed forcefully into a shop window, shattering the glass, and falling in a crumpled heap on the floor. "Stay there or I'll fucking hurt you!" Joe instructed sternly, before continuing on his way home. The suddenly subdued youths refrained from further confrontation, and he managed to get home without further incident, however, a few minutes after settling down with a beer, there was a knock at the door. On answering it Joe was confronted with an agitated man.

"Did you hit my son into a shop window?" he asked accusingly.

Joe could see he was angry but could also see he was intimidated by his stature.

"Yes I did, but before you say anything else let me explain something to you." Joe replied. "My name is Joe, I'm a Midlands heavyweight boxing champion and a paratrooper, and I don't appreciate being shouted at and threatened by a gang of shit stains, who think it's alright to abuse old ladies and spit in the street, when they should be out looking for a fucking job!"

The parent was taken aback. "Is that what happened? Were they causing trouble?" he asked.

Joe explained how the gang had been terrorising the locals and described how the night had transpired, much to annoyance of his visitor, who'd received a completely different version of events from his son. The bloke ended up apologising to Joe, and to show there were no hard feelings Joe invited him in and they had a beer together.

JONES NINE-TWO

In the army, when there are multiple people with the same surname, they are formally identified by the last two digits of their service number, to avoid confusion. In my platoon we had two Private Jones's, both also nicknamed "Jonah" so on any nominal rolls or taskings they were designated as Jones 92, and Jones 18. Eventually "Nine-Two" became the nickname for Jones 92, his actual name was Jay Jones but we already had a "JJ" so that was taken.

Nine-Two was a big bloke, with a background in Muay Thai kickboxing that he kept quiet about, but we discovered for ourselves when we saw him working out on a punchbag. A few of us were lifting weights in the upstairs gym one evening when we heard the sound of someone hitting the bag in the downstairs sports hall. Whoever was down there was whacking the hell out of it, the sound echoing through the old building. We walked to the edge of the balcony that overlooked the main gym floor and saw 92 casually throwing some loose combinations on the punchbag, effortlessly making it bend in half and swing wildly on its chain as he moved forwards, backwards and sideways smoothly. We had a ringer!

One night a group of us were out in town and our platoon sergeant, Tam had joined us for a beer. He was a mega bloke and well-liked by us all so when a man none of us recognised started talking to him, we watched vigilantly. As it turned out the bloke was from Tam's original recruit platoon, they'd actually joined Para Reg together, but he'd failed, and their paths hadn't crossed since. For a few minutes it was all going fine, but then the civilian started to get more and more animated as he spoke, grabbing Tam by the face and trying to alpha-male him. This didn't go unnoticed, and we quickly ended up forming a circle around them, ready to defend Tam. He didn't need us, he could look after himself, but as a sergeant it wasn't in his best interests to be fighting in a pub, and we didn't want him to put his career at risk. It got to a point where the idiot started having a go at Tam, accusing him of thinking he was a better man because he'd made it into the regiment. He was clearly insecure and winding himself up towards a physical attack. Without taking his eyes off his old mate, in a calm voice, no louder than normal conversation Tam spoke.

"Hit him Jonah."

Jones 92 was stood by Tam's side and responded immediately, punching the antagonist hard in the face and dropping him to the floor. A couple of the others grabbed hold of his shirt and dragged him outside through the front entrance, then down the alley at the side of the pub. We watched their silhouettes through the stained glass windows as they saw to his wounds, or should I say, saw to it that he got some wounds.

92's kickboxing was put to good use on another occasion, to gain entry to a building. Convinced his girlfriend was in mortal danger because she had not been out or answered her phone, a drunk 92 climbed a fire escape and prised open a window to get into her apartment block. Banging on the door urgently, he shouted for her to open it, and when he got no response kicked it hard several times, breaking the lock and damaging the doorframe as it swung open. On looking inside he saw a man he'd never seen before, standing in the hallway looking very worried. Also in the hallway were pictures on the wall, a lampshade, and a carpet he'd never seen before either. It was the wrong apartment; his girlfriend lived next-door. She didn't want to see him anymore after that.

BUBBA JIM

The most impressive specimen of a human being I have ever seen was a soldier from A Company, 3 PARA called "Bubba Jim." 365 days a year, he looked like he was preparing for a bodybuilding contest, and I don't mean an amateur one. He was an absolute beast. Even the blokes who were on steroids were nowhere near his level, and he was completely steroid free. As a new bloke, a lot of people are intimidating, but his physical presence was in a league of its own. I remember when Jim was winding up a friend of mine who'd joined the army from South Africa. I walked into the room to hear him asking him.

"Do you hate black people? I bet you do! I bet you've got slaves at home haven't you? I'm going to make you my slave you fucking racist!"

Jim couldn't hold in his laugh for long as my friend Rich stood there absolutely terrified, not knowing what to say or do. Jim burst into a laugh and bear hugged him tightly. "Only joking mate." he said.

I was as relieved as Rich, but he was shell-shocked for a while.

The first time I spoke to Jim was in a T.V room on a camp in Lydd, Kent. When I entered the room he was the only person in there, sitting in the second row of old, ragged, cushioned chairs watching the television. There were about thirty chairs, in five or six rows, and one crappy old T.V at the front that was probably donated by someone who'd upgraded to one with a remote control. Soldiers are often reluctant to sit in the front row of any audience or gathering, because in the army the front row is where the important people sit. The highest ranking officer usually sits in the middle of the front row, and the rest sit wherever they deem themselves worthy in a loose hierarchical order around him. The junior ranks normally fill up from the back, in order to keep as far away from the sensible people as possible, the senior ranks sit a couple of rows back from the front and the Sergeant Majors sit wherever the hell they want.

As a new bloke, I sat at the back of the T.V room to show respect. Even though Jim was a private too, he was much more senior than me and waiting to be promoted to lance corporal. He noticed me come in and we exchanged nods as I sat down quietly. After a couple of minutes I noticed his head turning around towards me slowly, and, expecting him to say something, I looked him in the eye as he faced me. Neither of us spoke and he returned his gaze to the telly. A short while later, he turned again, and once more I looked at him in anticipation, only for him to face forwards again in silence. A few seconds passed, and Jim did it again, this time though he spun his whole body round to speak.

"Steve why are you fucking staring at me?" he said sharply. He looked a bit freaked out.

"I'm not staring at you Jim." I replied.

Jim explained his logic. "Every time I turn around, you are watching me, it's fucking creepy mate!"

I found it strange that he seemed unnerved by me and justified myself. "I keep thinking you're going to say something Jim, so I look so I can hear you. I'm not staring at you, I'm watching the telly."

Jim patted the seat next to him. "Come and sit here you weirdo." He said, shaking his head. "Why would you sit over there by yourself anyway?"

I moved seats and we ended up chatting for a long time. He was a good bloke, I never heard a bad word said about him.

One thing he couldn't tolerate though was creepy crawlies. We were on a six week exercise in Botswana in 1994, spending most of the time based out of a tented camp in the middle of nowhere, in the bush. Right next to our camp lived a troop of Baboons and we'd see them most days. Back then I didn't even realise how dangerous they could be, but these ones just ignored us like we weren't even there, and we'd often see them patrolling the area, moving tactically in a very similar way to us. Sometimes they even did obstacle crossing drills like we did, across tracks and wadis. The other regular creatures to be found in abundance were Scorpions and Camel Spiders, and if you looked, you'd find them. The best thing to do was not look, because they didn't want you to find them and would leave you alone if you left them alone. It was important to check your kit before using it or wearing it, but apart from that, forget about them. One night the tent next to mine erupted in shouts, squeals and laughs as Jim hunted a camel spider that had crawled under one of the old fashioned camp-cots. Unable to relax until he knew it was dead he went on a one man search and destroy mission, and in his panic was launching cots into the air and across the tent while the blokes were still in them. Eventually he uncovered it and squashed it with a heavy object before returning to his own cot and getting his head down.

KNIFE MAN

Walking through Girdwood Camp in Northern Ireland one day, I couldn't help but notice a bloke crawling across the grass football pitch with a large knife between his teeth while getting blasted with a full size, high pressure fire hose, that was plugged into the sub-surface fire hydrant. Two Corporals were shouting words of encouragement to him as they directed the jet of water into his face. He'd obviously been there for a while because the pitch was flooded, and he looked exhausted. Like everyone else who saw it, I just carried on like it was normal, certain that someone was being stitched up, and not wanting to spoil it. The office I was heading to faced out to the pitch so when I got there I asked the blokes inside what was going on.

"He thinks he's going on an underwater knife fighting course." I was informed. "He's doing some pre-training to get ready for it." It turned out it was a new lad, who'd been wound up by the blokes in his platoon. They'd convinced him he'd been selected to attend the non-existent underwater knife fighting course and offered to help him prepare. He was the only bloke in the whole battalion who wasn't in on the joke.

As a kid, I had a couple of close encounters with knives, the first being when I was about eight years old. Exploring the local forest with my older brother and a few of his friends we stumbled upon another group of kids who were constructing a camp. These kids were older and bigger than us, and back then it was like some kind of unwritten rule that big kids beat up little kids if they didn't know each other. Camp site locations were top-secret and us walking into theirs as they built it with shovels, saws and knives was a massive faux pas. Knives in hand, they chased us through the woods, shouting angrily, and despite being the youngest and smallest in our group I was at the front, as we fled for our lives to the safety of our estate.

My brother had an alter ego when we were teenagers that would only come to life in front of me, and a few of my mates. "Knife Man" was for the most part a comedy character, who jokingly threatened me with large knives from our kitchen drawer. He'd wave them around in my face and throw them in my general direction in an attempt to scare, rather than hurt me. Sometimes it would get a bit out of hand though, and I'd be forced to run, getting a five to ten second head start before he'd begin the chase. I'd run out through the back door and sprint up the lane behind our house, encouraging any friends that were visiting to follow on. Many times a knife would strike the ground behind or beside me or go flying past in the air as he launched them with a manic laugh. To this day I have a small scar on my hand where he got too close while I was covering my face. To be fair I did stab him once too though. I threw a dart at him as he ran up some stairs and it embedded itself into the top of his skull.

The last time he turned into Knife Man was not a joke. I was about seventeen and him nineteen, when we had an argument in the house, and I shoved him. Being a fair bit heavier than him I sent him flying, and he stumbled sideways, falling over, and banging his head off a windowsill. On standing up he walked quickly towards the kitchen in a rage. I knew exactly where he was going and took myself into the living room, closing the door behind me and wedging my foot into the bottom of it, as I pressed it closed. I heard the unmistakeable sound of the cutlery drawer being yanked open as he went to get a knife and heard my mum shout at him to put it down. As I stood behind the door he started smashing into it with the end of a roller blind that was lying around, putting a large hole into the wooden panels. Not sure if he had the knife or not I stayed where I was, and my brother quickly realised he couldn't get to me and left. He had a right temper!

CHAPTER FOUR

Home & Fashion

LIVING CONDITIONS

When you've been in the army it makes you laugh how people whinge about their living conditions sometimes. The blokes don't complain, but they are regularly treated worse than convicted criminals and people held in detention facilities. Living conditions in the military can be a bit hit and miss. When I was sent to 3 PARA in 1994 we lived in Bruneval Barracks, Montgomery Lines, Aldershot. Apparently those accommodation blocks were condemned as unsuitable for human habitation not long after their construction in the 1970's, and a well-known rumour was that the architect was in prison for another project he'd been involved with. They were great to live in from a soldiers perspective though; sociable, basic, and hard wearing, but from a health and safety perspective they were not so good. There was only one way in and out, with no emergency exits. The toilets and ablutions were in the middle of the block, with no ventilation system and there was no fire plan. Loads of the windows had been installed by the blokes after they'd been smashed. Most weekends you'd see someone carrying a pane of glass from town, on their way to fix their own window before it would be discovered on Monday morning. It was rumoured that some of the windows had PE4 plastic explosive sealing the windows, where it had been used to replace the original, damaged window putty. Some of the blocks also had big cracks in the walls that ran from the ground, to the roof on the second floor.

In 1995 I moved to Connaught Barracks in Dover and my Company, D Company, was allocated the Transit Accommodation block, which was normally only used for short term occupancy. I lived in there for four years. At weekends they used to turn off the heating and hot water, so we'd have our last hot shower on Friday afternoon and cold one's after that until Monday morning. In 1997 I went to West Belfast, Northern Ireland and lived in a tiny four-man room in a Mortar Shelter. It had two bunkbeds with a gap in the middle and we all had a box under the bottom bunk for our kit. Luckily, I shared that room with some great blokes, so we had a good laugh.

In 1999 I went to the Pathfinders, and we moved to Wattisham Airfield near Ipswich, Suffolk. In that camp we lived in portacabins. Water used to run down the inside of the corridor walls during heavy rain, and some of the fire exits couldn't be opened from the inside. I raised this with a maintenance man once and he said. "Yes, but you can get in though, right?"

"Yes, but if there's a fire I think I'll probably want to get fucking out!" I explained.

In 2004 I moved to Colchester with the Pathfinders, and we were accommodated in an old office block that had been repurposed. We were on tour in Afghanistan when that building was demolished, and when we came back the blokes had to sleep on the floor of our offices, because there was no accommodation for them anymore.

When we were in Kabul, Afghanistan in 2002 we spent some time in a compound that the Royal Marines had taken over as a patrol base. Space was limited and we were allocated one small room which they took us to.

"Sorry about the mess. You'll have to clean it out lads, every room in the compound was the same when we got here, filthy!" the Marine Colour Sergeant told us.

Inside there was human excrement on the floor in every corner from when the compound had been empty, and locals had used it as a public toilet. We got rid of it, and later that night we were sleeping on that floor. It could have been worse, some of the rooms had discarded hypodermic needles in them too. That sort of thing was common in Kabul, sometimes people wouldn't even look for somewhere private, they would just stop on the pavement and take a crap right there and then. One thing you never saw though was toilet paper. Strange place.

PACK YOUR BAGS

When you have to carry everything that you've packed in your bergan on your back, for days on end, up hills, down hills, across marshes, through forests, and over walls, you learn to prioritise what is essential and what is a nicety. The first time I went out on an overnight exercise in recruit training, I followed the packing list to the letter, but still got it wrong. Our kit was all laid out for an inspection, and I remember one of the corporals stopping next to mine and bending down to grab something.

"Who's is this?" he shouted, holding up a full size can of shaving foam. "Which mong is taking a months' worth of shaving foam for one night in the field?"

The inspection hadn't even started yet, and we were still running around getting things ready, but I heard him, and knew it was mine.

"If nobody claims it, then I'm taking it!" he said. "Absolutely no need to be carrying shit like that!"

I kept quiet, he could have it. I'd rather buy another one than get beasted.

One of my Depot corporals had been one of the youngest soldiers in 3 PARA to deploy to the Falkland Islands in 1982, and every now and then he'd tell us a story about his experiences. Corporal Mac was an imposing figure, a big, broad chested man, who was fiercely proud of his regiment, and was firm, but fair with us recruits. On parades he always stood out because he had more medals than everyone else. Back then the majority of soldiers we saw only had one medal, the Northern Ireland General Service Medal. Corporal Mac had two more in addition to that; one from The Falklands War, and one from a United Nations, Cyprus tour. One day he was telling us about the long march across the Falklands that he'd been a part of, explaining how the men had carried ridiculous weights, across fifty miles of horrendous terrain. Loaded down with their own personal kit and weapons, many of the paras also carried lots of extra ammunition, including machine gun and mortar rounds. Cpl Mac told us that the blokes ditched everything that wasn't vital to the mission, including spare clothing, rations they could live without, and even took wrappers from food to reduce their load. One of the recruits questioned the logic behind removing wrappers.

"They weigh next to nothing." he said. "Would it even be worth it Corporal?"

Corporal Mac answered him sincerely. "It all adds up lads. Plus, it's less rubbish to carry around. We binned everything we didn't need, so we could carry more ammunition into battle." he told us, finishing with a rhyme:

"Bullets and water,

Off to the slaughter."

He was a great instructor, and his credibility was unquestionable.

After a few years in the army you've worked out what kit you can, and can't do without, how much food you can get by on, and how much water you need to stay adequately hydrated in various environments. Everyone is different, so sometimes the advice from another soldier might not fit your requirements, while other times they will give you a top-tip, a golden nugget of information that they've learned through their own hard earned experience, that helps you immeasurably. In my opinion the best places to learn this stuff are the jungle, and on operations. The jungle is an extremely harsh environment where regardless of the weather, you are literally dripping wet all day. Because of the humidity, sweat cannot evaporate from your skin, so beads of it coat every inch of your body, dripping from your wrinkled finger tips in a steady trickle, if you let your arm hang down. Rainy season, or dry season, your clothes are constantly soaked like you've just been caught in a torrential downpour. Even in the relative coolness of the night, any form of physical exertion will quickly get you perspiring again. This is why you have a dry set of clothing just for sleeping in that you change into every night at the last moment, before getting your head down, and replace with your cold, wet ones first thing in the morning as soon as you get up.

I endured a horrendous lesson on equipment-packing in the jungle once. I was on a course in Belize and one of the Jungle Warfare Instructors from a regiment I'd never heard of gave us the lesson, using his own personal kit for demonstration. Me and my good friend Ginge were sat next to each other, elbowing one another in the ribs and trying not to laugh as this lunatic started pulling bits of kit from his pouches and unconvincingly justifying them. Pulling out a metal mug, he explained that he preferred it to a mess tin, because it did the same job, except you could also drink out of it. We all agreed with that advice as it was what we already used, it made perfect sense. However he then pulled out an issued, black plastic mug.
"Black mug. Great for drinking your brew out of." he said, receiving a few raised eyebrows from us in the audience. Carrying two things for one purpose was bad enough, but then he went even further, taking another drinking receptacle from a pouch, this time a tiny, folding, rubber cup.
"Folding cup. Great for a small drink, or for a drink on the move." he informed us, as he mimed the actions of withdrawing it from his pocket, scooping up some water and drinking it, commentating, "During a river crossing, you can just pull it out, grab a drink, then put it away." It probably was a good way to get a quick drink, but it was a brilliant way of contracting a water-borne disease like cryptosporidiosis, giardia, or cholera. The length of comms cord he had, was a useless, mass entanglement of green garden twine that resembled a birds nest. In our kit we had fishing reels with fifty metres of strong cordage, tightly wound onto

them. He also had the good old torch with the end taped over and just a tiny pinprick hole for light to escape. This is a top tip in many military tactics and survival books that sounds great, but in my experience is impossible in real life. His kit looked like it had been packed by a ten year old army cadet, who'd read too many copies of Combat & Survival magazine, then spent his pocket money at a Walter Mitty jumble sale, whilst high on crack cocaine. I remember that lesson only because it was so bad.

On operations you quickly get rid of everything you don't absolutely need. The weight of live ammunition, including grenades, and spare rounds for machine guns, plus body armour, and helmets soon adds up. Knowing that your ability to move fast will increase your chance of survival in a firefight, is a good incentive to reduce the weight you carry. Things like your favourite knife that you've had for years and use for making traps in the forest get removed. The tiny spare torch you normally wear around your neck for those spontaneous night time jobs is left behind, and your big metal spoon gets replaced by a smaller, lighter, plastic one. Other space and weight saving measures include:

- Sawing a pencil in half
- Tearing out a few blank pages from a notebook instead of carrying the whole thing
- Wearing the same underwear for lengthy periods rather than carry spare
- Cutting maps down to size and discarding any parts not required
- Cutting off parts of clothing that do not get used such as epaulettes and inside pockets
- Cutting down toothbrush handles
- Swapping a good sleeping bag for a far inferior, but smaller and lighter one

INAPPROPRIATELY DRESSED

A few months after retiring from the army I was out with my dog, when we got caught in a torrential downpour of rain. Against my better judgement I did something that I hadn't done for twenty-seven years, something that would have turned my stomach as a young paratrooper. But I was a civvy now, pushing new boundaries and exploring the freedoms it offered. It was actually a moment of enlightenment, and to my pleasant surprise I didn't burst into flames or get struck by lightning. The rain passed and I continued on my way to meet my friend Will, who I told about my discovery.

"I put my hood up a minute ago." I declared proudly.

Will nodded, seemingly not all that impressed.

"It's actually a good bit of kit." I explained. "Not only does it keep your head dry, but it also stops the rain going down the back of your neck as well."

He looked at me like I was an idiot. "Yes Steve, I know that already mate." He said dryly. "Everybody knows that already."

In the paras we never wore hoods. Putting up a hood was a sure sign that someone was monging it, they'd switched off, given up. We were rightly taught in Depot that hoods impaired your hearing and restricted your field of view, wearing a hood could prevent you from identifying the enemy, and compromise the security of your team. The brim of floppy hats is always trimmed by paratroopers too. Other units often make comments, saying that it's stupid because the brim protects you from the Sun, but we also like to protect ourselves from the enemy, who might be above us on a hill, or a booby trap that could be hanging from a tree. Trimming back the brim increases your field of view and enhances the security of your team.

Gloves were another massive no-no for most people in battalion too. They hampered weapon handling, especially magazine changes, which require some dexterity to undo and fasten ammunition pouches. When they were used, normally in extreme weather conditions, the finger tips were often cut off, but they were never worn unless it was at least minus ten degrees, with a wind chill factor of minus two hundred. Gore-tex trousers were treated like some kind of kryptonite, nobody ever wore them. It was crazy because we all carried them, and they were always on the packing list. The one time I wore them in 3 PARA was building snow caves in Norway, where we all wore full Gore-tex because we were crawling around in snow.

In the winter of 2000 I was on a promotion course in Brecon, Wales, where the weather is notoriously bad. During the early part of the course my instructor noticed I wasn't wearing Gore-tex to the classroom when the others in my section were. I didn't see the point in mucking about, putting it on and taking it off for the sake of a sixty second run across the camp. The classroom was warm and dry, why bother? I didn't realise his interpretation of this until our first day on the ranges on Sennybridge Training Area, where it only rains once a year (It starts at 0001hrs on the 1st of Jan and continues until 2359hrs 31st December!) There were about fifty of us on that range, and just before firing was to commence it started raining.

"Right, everyone stop what you're doing and get your Gore-tex on now." Called out my instructor wisely. "We're here all day, you don't want to be piss-wet through!"

I was already thinking the same, and about to pull my jacket from my daysac when he continued unexpectedly.

"Corporal Brown doesn't wear Gore-tex, for whatever reason," he declared. "And that's his choice, but the rest of you, get it on."

I was standing with my mate Stu from 3 PARA, and we looked at each other in surprise.

"Eh?" he said. "What's that all about?"

I shook my head. "I don't know, but he's seen me right off there!" We'd done a couple of courses together and were drinking buddies, so Stu knew me pretty well. "You do wear Gore-tex!" he stated.

"Apparently not anymore mate." I replied. "Now it looks like I've said I don't wear it, so if I do, it looks like I've jacked!" I was gutted, that course was three months long, and all through the winter, whatever I did, I'd have to stick to it, but I just couldn't bare the thought of the instructor getting one up on me.

Stu was putting his jacket on. "What you gonna do mate?"

"Fuck it. Skin's waterproof!" I said. Like an idiot, I did that whole course without putting it on.

During that same course there is a phase called "Attack Week", where you spend the entire week practicing section and platoon attacks. Inevitably, on most of the ranges the obvious route to the enemy positions is through bogs, mud, streams, and rivers. Sometimes ranges will have a river running through them that isn't even necessarily the best approach, but you will still be getting in it either way. A friend of mine who'd done the course the previous winter gave me some advice before I went on it.

"During attack week, wear jungle boots." He suggested.

I was surprised at that because jungle boots are designed for hot climates, they are not waterproof at all and have no lining to the leather, in fact they actually have holes in them to let water out.

"Surely they'd be too cold?" I queried.

He explained his logic. "You're in and out of water all day anyway, so your feet are soaked no matter what, but jungle boots are lighter, and they'll dry overnight. Gore-tex boots will stay wet, and they're mega heavy."

It made sense. I took his advice and wore my jungle boots, explaining my reasons why to a few intrigued people on the drive to the ranges, who looked at me inquisitively. They weren't convinced, and the second we crossed the cattle grid and entered the training area, neither was I. The ground was covered in a thin layer of snow and the puddles along the road were frozen solid. On the descent to our drop off point our four-ton truck started sliding down the hill, going sideways momentarily before the driver regained control and stopped. We bailed out after that, climbing over the tailgate, jumping off, and opting to walk the rest of the way. My feet were freezing. The next day I wore proper boots.

PARA REG T-SHIRTS

As a Private soldier in A Company, 3 PARA my wardrobe contained thirteen Parachute Regiment t-shirts and one seldom-worn civilian one. Para Reg t-shirts were great and came in a selection of colours; green or maroon, and they were multi-functional. You could wear them for fitness, you could wear them on exercise, (green variant) and you could wear them down town as your "casual attire." They were also a good way to identify friend from foe. If Para Reg blokes were fighting each other, then you could determine which side to join in with by the battalion markings. If Para Reg blokes were fighting anyone else you knew to attack those not wearing Para Reg tops.

In the 1980's two soldiers were arrested after the police came onto camp in Aldershot and took them into custody. A couple of nights before their arrest a robbery had taken place just outside Aldershot, and the police had closed in on them quickly. CCTV footage of the crime was obtained by the investigating officers, and they had noticed something quite distinctive about the clothing the robbers wore. Both were dressed in t-shirts with a Parachute Regiment cap badge, and the words "*C Company 3 PARA*" on them. Those cunning Hampshire Police took a punt and visited the Company Headquarters of C Company, 3 PARA with the footage, and asked the Sergeant Major and Officer Commanding. "Do you know these two men?"
There's only so much you can do to cover for your blokes, so the two men were sent for and promptly arrested.

By the late 90's entry into nightclubs wearing Para Reg t-shirts was not permitted in most establishments, including Nu-Age nightclub in Dover. Sometimes we'd get caught out, because we'd pop into town during the day for a quick pint wearing our scruffs and end up staying out all day. The barracks was at the top of a steep hill, and it was impossible to walk up without breaking a sweat, so going back to get changed was not an ideal option. Sometimes you could get away with turning your top inside-out, but that didn't work on the embroidered ones. One night, a bloke from Support Company called Sam King found himself in this exact predicament and with nobody wearing a jumper he could borrow to cover his t-shirt he tried another innovative technique.

"I'll give you ten quid for your top." He said, to a tramp sitting in a shop doorway drinking cans of extra strength lager.

The homeless man declined the offer, shaking his head and waving Sam away dismissively. Sam took out his wallet and upped his offer, holding the cash out in front of the man.

"How about twenty quid then?" he bid.

Still not interested in selling his clothing and dignity, the tramp again refused.

Sam had had enough of the bartering. Reaching down he grabbed the t-shirt at the waist and yanked it upwards. "You had your chance mate!" he said, as he pulled it over the head of the shocked homeless man and walked off with it. He put that free t-shirt on, and wore it to the nightclub, spending the £20 on alcohol instead.

New regimental t-shirts are sometimes made for special occasions, operational tours, or big exercises. They always have a nice big Para Reg cap badge, and sometimes have a cartoon or corny quote on them. Some of the blokes love them, and wear them with pride, while others loathe them. As a young soldier I thought they were great. As an old git, they're not my cup of tea anymore unless they are simple and discrete. The very first time I met my mother-in-law I was wearing a maroon t-shirt, with a cap badge, and the words:

"Rather my sister in a whorehouse, than my brother a craphat!" Luckily she didn't notice, and I only realised a few years later, when I saw a photo from that day.

I donated my Airborne Forces 94' t-shirt that I bought from the "Rat Pit" pub in Aldershot to the Pathfinders bar twenty years after I bought it. On that was written:

"Roll on down to the Rat Pit
The beer's flat
The company's crap
The music's contagious
The price's outrageous
The bar staff atrocious
The women ferocious
It's a paratrooper's paradise."Other designs have included:

"On the eighth day, God created paratroopers.
And The Devil stood to attention!"

"Paratroopers Wanted:
We are looking for hard drinking, good looking, tough fighting, special lovers.
There are a lot of fat, ugly, boring people out there.
If you are one of them, do not bother reading any more.
Just f**k off.
As a paratrooper, you'll have countless fights with your fellow soldiers. You will win.
What's more, you will enjoy active service with some of the finest ladies the world can offer.
Lucky them.
If you'd like to have a bash at being a paratrooper and can hold your own at drinking, forget the devastating implications for your girlfriends – APPLY NOW."

"Only God can judge the Taliban.
We just arrange the meeting."

"Our training is tough, our standards are high.
We are the Paras, Gods of the sky.
Maroon is our colour, our cap badge our pride.
Enemies know, there's nowhere to hide.
We are elite, not people, machines.
From husbands to brothers,
To sons in their teens.
We risk our lives, to the people we pledge,
Airborne for life, we are The Reg."

IMPROVISED CLOTHING

One morning after a heavy night in Dover I woke up in a strange bed with no idea of where I was. Lying on my side at the edge of the mattress I noticed an obvious wet patch on the carpet and bits of white fluff scattered everywhere like a swan had exploded in there. I also noticed I was wearing a big piece of white fluffy material around my neck; it had a big tear in it that I'd pushed my head through. Slowly I began piecing together memory snapshots from the night before and a wave of awkward embarrassment washed over me. During the night I'd woken up and opened up my daysac to retrieve a sweatshirt, discarding anything else I pulled out across the room. When I failed to find it, I went into a drawer at the bottom of the bed and pulled out another jumper, but the bed was wet, so I sat on the edge, folded my arms, and tried to sleep sitting down. Or that's what I thought at the time in my paralytic, half asleep state. In reality, I'd been ripping out the stuffing from my pillow, torn a length off the bottom of the duvet, ripped a hole in it and popped it over my head. The girl who's house it was had woken up to see me sitting on her bed, wearing a big, fluffy scarf.

"What are you doing?" she asked, herself also very drunk.

"I'm fucking freezing." I replied, rocking slightly like a complete lunatic.

She must have wondered what the hell was going on. "Get in bed then." She said.

"It's soaking wet." I snapped. Pointing behind me blindly I accused some people who I imagined were also in the room "One of them pricks has spilled a drink!"

She patted the bed and felt the wet sheet. "Have you pee'd on my bed?" she asked worriedly.

I pointed behind me again and repeated my claim. "No. One of them lot spilled a drink!"

"Just lie down but avoid the wet bit." She said.

I did and woke up a few hours later to the carnage.

On a survival course in 1994 we were provided with a pile of waste materials to use in the construction of shelters and clothing. Amongst the rubbish was sandbags, plastic bags, bits of rope and empty bottles. In my team we decided to utilise the hessian material of the sandbags to fabricate some clothing and fashioned hoods, gloves, face masks and waistcoats. We used our knives to cut the material to size and sewed pieces together using the heart lines from paracord. The items were crude but practical, and we all ended up with additional layers to take onto the moor with us, along with the smoked food we'd prepared. One day just before sunset on the evasion phase, I woke up from a short nap, shivering from the cold. My team and I had concealed ourselves in some tall grass, heather and gorse and tried to get some sleep before setting off on our nightly fifteen kilometre traipse across Dartmoor. I brushed the grass and foliage off of me and sat up, watching the others do the same. We were all feeling sorry for ourselves; it was freezing cold, wet, windy, and none of us had really slept. I looked at my friend Rich and burst out laughing; he looked absolutely ridiculous. His hessian hat looked like a cross between a beige Ku Klux Klan hood and a Bishops hat, his mask was a piece of sacking with three holes cut into it for his eyes and mouth, and his gloves were just stumps, with no fingers or thumbs. He looked at me and reacted the same way; I looked as stupid as him, we all did, and we sat there for a couple of minutes laughing at each other like a bunch of escaped mental patients. To be fair, it wasn't supposed to be a fashion parade, and our poorly made accessories did make us a little bit more comfortable.

SCRUFFY LIZARDS

The Verve were a big band in the mid-nineties and in 1997, at the height of their popularity, I went to a concert of theirs in Brixton with a couple of mates from 3 PARA. Andy had heard about it on the radio and asked me and another mate Ginge if we fancied going. We were all privates and were half way through our first promotion course in Pirbright called Drill and Duties, so we needed a bit of time to relax. It was Friday afternoon when Andy suggested the idea, and the concert was that night, so his plan was to buy tickets from touts at the train station or outside the venue. As soon as we got off the train there were ticket touts everywhere, and we bought some within a few minutes then made our way to Brixton Academy. The Verve's bestselling album, Urban Hymns, which I had on CD had only been released a couple of months earlier, so people were really excited to see them live and it was heaving inside. We got ourselves some beer, then went into the downstairs auditorium, with Andy leading the way to the mosh pit, where we stood and waited. After a small performance by a warm-up band the announcer started to build up the tension before welcoming The Verve onto stage. Considering the state of the band members; who resembled a young version of the Rolling Stones, except skinnier, scruffier, uglier, and twice as experienced with drugs, there were a lot of attractive women in the crowd. For a few seconds, the crowd went quiet as we waited for them to appear, and a woman excitedly shouted out "We love you Richard." Obviously, she was a fan of the lead singer Richard Ashcroft, who came out first. At that point, right before the crowd started cheering, Andy leapt up in the air, using an unsuspecting Ginge's shoulders to gain height, pointed to Richard Ashcroft, and screamed at the top of his voice "You scruffy bastard!"

Nobody saw that coming, and there were quite a few dirty looks from people as the rest of the band came on stage, taking up their positions behind microphones and instruments. Ashcroft began to address the crowd and it went quiet once more as they listened to the superstar speak.

"You fucking lizard!" came the next shout from Andy, interrupting the singer mid-sentence and prompting him to get on with the show. I don't know if it was supposed to be a mosh-pit where we were, but it turned into one when Andy started shoving people around, and we all joined in. That was the one and only concert I ever went to, but it was a good crack. After the show we went into London to carry on drinking, missed the last train back, and ended up sleeping on the floor in Waterloo train station until the first morning train. Ginge went on to have a long, exemplary career in the army, promoting through the ranks to Regimental Sergeant Major and then commissioning as an officer. Andy was a highly respected soldier, especially known for his jungle warfare expertise. Sadly, Andy died in 2016 after falling through a roof in Thailand. RIP mate.

CHAPTER FIVE

Banter/ Psychological Warfare

WATCH THE LOG

I love hearing stories about the stupid things blokes have done in the past. Making a silly mistake in front of other soldiers is devastating, because you know they are going to:

1. Mock you.
2. Tell everyone else, and
3. Never forget.

In my first platoon in A Company 3 PARA, there was a softly spoken, Scottish bloke called James. He was a Private that had served four or five years and already completed two tours in Northern Ireland by the time I got there. Apparently, during a patrol through the countryside in Northern Ireland, the person in front of him had turned around and quietly said, "Watch the log!" Pointing to a small fallen tree in their pathway.

In the darkness, a log had almost tripped up one of the other soldiers at the front, so he'd warned off the man behind about the obstacle, and the message had been passed back all the way to James, the last man. A few minutes later the patrol came to a halt to conduct a map check when they realised James was missing. After a short wait, they retraced their steps and found him kneeling next to the fallen tree, watching it intently with unblinking eyes, weapon in the shoulder. The Patrol Commander was perplexed.

"What the fuck are you doing?" he asked.

"I was told to watch the log Sergeant." James replied.

You can't fault that kind of obedience from a young soldier. Their job is not to question their orders but execute them. I wonder how long he would have stayed there, and what he was expecting that log to do.

When I was in Northern Ireland, a friend of mine was on duty in a sentry tower when he was startled by some banging on the window from the outside. On inspection he realised it was one of the blokes peering through from the outside.

"What the fuck are you doing?!" he shouted, alarmed to see somebody on the outside of the security post.

Another good friend of mine called "Stoddy" shouted back, in his thick Cockney accent. "How do I get in there?" he asked.

The man already inside was stumped, the entrance was blatantly obvious, a ladder at the base of the small tower led straight to the sentry position via a hatchway.

"Use the fucking ladder!" he yelled, pointing downwards.

Stoddy disappeared, entering the observation post a few moments later to take over watch.

Over the following days several of us looked at that tower, but none of us could figure out how the confusion had arisen, or how Stoddy had climbed outside the perimeter. Mad as a box of frogs, but a mega bloke.

On another occasion, from a different sentry tower in that camp, a new bloke from B Company alerted the Operations Room that an IRA attack was imminent. Noticing a small airplane high in the sky above camp, he came to the conclusion that it could be the IRA, about to launch a high-altitude, low opening (HALO) parachute mission onto our base. There was no denying it, he'd said it over the radio and been heard by everyone on that channel, including the duty officer on watchkeeper duty. Imagine the kudos that the IRA would have received if they had launched an attack like that. It would have been absolute suicide, but they'd be legends, dead legends.

LOVE LETTERS

Receiving letters is great for morale, and before everyone had mobile phones you would either queue at the phone box on camp or send and receive letters to communicate with your parents or girlfriend. Even today, because of the cyber threat, letters can sometimes be the only way to communicate. A letter from a girlfriend or wife, especially one that had been sprayed with perfume was always a good boost, but letters from the blokes were a different beast. I kept loads of the one's I received from my mates, and today I could probably use them in a court of law to prove allegations of bullying, harassment, stalking, intimidation, death threats, and hate crimes. They were good for morale too; morale of the bloke writing them, the bloke receiving them, and everyone else who they'd be passed around to for a bit of entertainment. The harsher, the better, with no rules or constraints, and nobody was off-limits, they read like pure hate mail. I loved both writing and receiving them.

The following is a letter I received from one of my best mates Scotty, when we were in Northern Ireland in 1997. We were deployed to different areas so apart from the occasional call to an ops room, we kept in touch via letters. This letter was for me and several of the other blokes at my location and did not have the luxury of "spell check." I've deliberately copied the original text exactly how it was written, for comedy value and added pictures from the original letter that accompanied the writing.

For some context:
My southern, Aylesbury accent got me accused of being a Cock-

ney, and I had a girlfriend who had gone to live in Moscow.

McFadden had recently been promoted to Lance Corporal and had a female acquaintance in Dover, who we said had a hairy top lip.

Jonah had got injured and put on some weight. Scotty had never met his sister.

Tyler was from Newent, near Gloucester and had a lean physique.

Mick was a good looking bloke with some Chinese heritage, and he had hair. The picture he received was a medical red cross symbol:

Steve Geezer
looser Cockney
Gimp From
Alsbury
Brown

Geezer
you Fucking looser, Pathetic excuse for a paratrooper. Get a grip of
your Cockney life you gimp. Stax of chicks for you brown O.F.R

L/cpl McFADDEN
Mates Stax now he's a L/cpl, you Might WaNNa Send this to Jane L/
cpl Mcfadden And tell her to get a wash the fucking lizzard, face lift

and to go to weight watchers the fat whore.

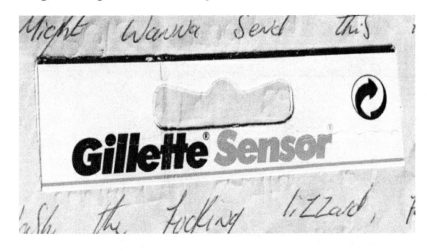

The lot of you are Fucking loosers Bunch of Joe Crow Hats who has no idea of soldier-ing Need any tips contact Scotty By the call "Scotty Scotty Scotty"

FAT Boy
– CAN oNly Mean oNe thing lose weight you Fat bitch every heard of Jenny Craig you ugly one ab gay lover of Stu Tyler. You Sister is a ugly Dwalf from leadbury and she love come. get a wash you stinking obeast 40 minutes miler CFT king Take Note – Ginster Pie Man

Now who CaN this be Tyler From Gloster.
You Frog eye'd ugly big eyed rubbed lipped looser. Son of Rosie West
move somewhere else you skiNNy grave digger.

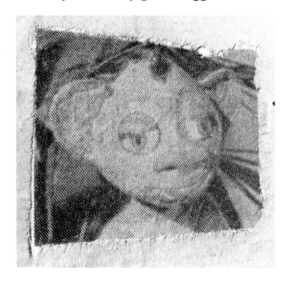

Mick
Take note Chinese elvis because your gonna need it boyo

One thing left to say I'm the best and chick love me Your all fucking
homeboys and love cock

The following letter was sent to me shortly after leaving 3 PARA and joining the Pathfinders. The blokes were actually really pleased that I'd passed the course, joining Ginge Parker, another soldier from our platoon, who'd passed the previous year.

For context:

The Pathfinders were specialists in covert reconnaissance.

Croc Holmes was a sergeant in 3 PARA with an impressive moustache:

CLASSIFIED

Geezmong hows it going you fucking stinking PATHFINDER scum bag hows your best mate Parker ginge type. I've just been down to the Urinal and I've found my old dear kicking fucking out of some old slapper called Brownie Mrs type. So I Said what the fucks going on. Your old dear had only been drinking out the urinal again. I Telt that bitch that's My old dears turf and to back the fuck up.

I thought I'd get you a prezzie for Crimbo it's called the P Fister Do it your self discuise kit.

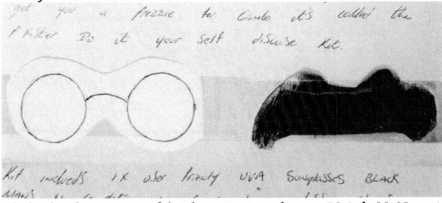

Kit inclueds 1 x user frieNly UVA Sunglasses BLAck MaNs x 1 complete, Croc Homes tash x 1 complete. Use this kit well and I hope it brings you Joy and good will. And I hope it gives you as much fun and happiness to you as it did for me.

WITH FRIENDS LIKE US WHO NEEDS ENEMIES?

I was always a bit of a bastard really. One day, when I was about thirteen or fourteen years old, I was on my way home after school when I knocked on the door of an old mate. We'd recently fallen out over some trivia, and I saw an opportunity to get him in trouble. His mum was quite posh and extremely strict. I knocked the door and she answered.

"Hello, is Ben there please?" I asked. I knew he wasn't, I'd seen him hanging around with some other kids at the back of school. She hated him being called Ben. "Benjamin isn't home from school yet." she told me sternly.

I feigned disappointment. "Damn it! I was really hoping he'd be home." I paused for a moment before continuing the act. "Not to worry, I'll see him tomorrow."

His mum offered to help. "Do you want to leave a message?" she asked.

Ben didn't smoke, and neither did I, but that just added to the fun.

"The thing is." I bluffed. "I asked Ben to look after my cigarettes earlier because I was sent to see the headmaster, and I just wanted to get them back." I paused once more. She'd already be annoyed just by the idea he'd held onto them. "Mind you, knowing Ben, he's probably smoked them all by now anyway." I said.

She took the bait. "What do you mean!? Benjamin doesn't

smoke!" she snapped.

I walked away guiltily. "I'm sorry, I didn't mean to get him in trouble." I lied.

She was livid, and he got a right grilling when he got home.

I properly stitched up another mate called Ian once. We were doing a ten-week bricklaying course in High Wycombe and used to get the train there and back every day. We'd been friends since school so knew each other pretty well. He had a tendency to fall asleep on the return train in the afternoon, and I had a tendency to leave him on there, sneaking off quietly when we got to our station. I'd look forward to the next morning to find out how far he'd got on the route back to London before waking up. One day his girlfriend was waiting on the platform as our train pulled in, I'd never met her before, but he'd told me about her plenty enough. They had a quick hug and kiss before Ian introduced us. "This is my mate Steve." He said, gesturing towards me. "Steve, this is my girlfriend…"

I butted in before he could finish and grabbed her hand to shake it.

"Hello Claire." I said confidently. "I already know your name, he talks about you all the time." I knew full well her name was Sarah.

To my delight, she was immediately pissed off. "What!? Who the hell is Claire? My name's Sarah!" she snapped.

It was too easy. "Yeah right! I know it's Claire. Who do you think helped him write your Valentine's Day card?" I said convincingly. I also knew she'd been upset when he didn't give her a card a few weeks before.

Slapping his face, she shouted. "Who the fuck is Claire!?"

He was like a rabbit caught in the headlights. "Don't listen to him, he's lying! He pleaded. "Tell her you're joking you idiot!"

I skulked off, doing my best to act uncomfortable. "Yeah, sorry, I didn't want to start an argument." I said, and left them to it, feeling quite pleased with myself.

The next morning he told me it had taken him ages to calm her down and assure her it was a wind up.

"Why would you do that?" he asked.

"Because it's funny." I replied. It was funny. For me.

In 3 PARA while waiting in a pub called The Castle for one of the blokes to arrive, we decided to wind him up once he got there. That's how it normally works, if you're not there to defend yourself, you become the target. Scotty walked in, got a beer and joined us at the pool table in the back of the pub. We left it for a few minutes, so it didn't look suspicious, then Shaun started.

"Mate, we didn't know about Julie, we only just heard. What are you going to do?" he asked, feigning concern.

Scotty was confused. "What am I going to do about what?" he replied.

Jones 92 joined in. "I told you to be careful with her mate! She's trouble that one!"

I backed them up too. "Are you even sure it's yours?" I said. "I'd get that checked out if I was you!"

Scotty was getting wound up with us all talking in riddles. "What are you dicks talking about?" he snapped.

"The baby!" Shaun answered. "Julie told us about the baby!"

"I can't believe you never told us mate." Jones 92 said disappointedly.

Scotty was having none of it at first, but the more everyone backed up the story of how we'd seen his on/off girlfriend in town, and she'd told us all about it, the more we reeled him in. He soon became quite convinced that she had told us she was pregnant, but was hoping she was bluffing, or that it was someone else's baby. He sunk several beers in rapid succession, then disappeared without telling anyone he was going. After a short, brisk walk he arrived at Julie's house and banged on the door urgently. She was surprised to see him, they normally only saw each other on drunken nights out.

"Is it true?" he asked hastily.

"Is what true?" Julie replied ignorantly. Oblivious to the false information he'd been given.

"Just tell me if it's mine!" Scotty demanded.

Julie stood in silence, perplexed.

Scotty spelled it out. "Is the baby mine or not?!"

"What the hell are you talking about? What baby?" she quizzed, and at that point he knew he'd been stitched up like a kipper.

Stood on the doorstep he looked skywards and shouted. "Baaastaaaards!"

FUN AND GAMES

As a new bloke or "Crow" in a Para Battalion you can expect to be called upon at any given moment, to provide entertainment for the senior blokes in your Platoon or Company. For the most part it's just a bit of fun that everyone has done in the early days of Battalion life. One of the games is "Stoneman Racing" and is normally played during breaks between lessons or range practices when there is a plentiful supply of small stones. The pebble strewn ranges of the Kent coast at Hythe and Lydd, or Lydd and Hythe, depending on your Battalion were the perfect setting for this. Crows would tie off the ends of their shirt sleeves and trouser legs, secure any zips and buttons, tuck their shirts into their trousers, and then have their clothing filled to bursting point with small stones. Hardly able to move because of their immobilised limbs and sheer weight, new blokes are assisted to a start line and race each other across a set distance, each representing their Section or Platoon for a chance at glory. Inevitably they will fall over as they attempt to sprint, cheered on by the excited spectators which leads to the best part of all, watching them try to get back up. If you've never tried standing up without bending your arms and legs, try it, it's impossible, but funny to watch.

Another game is "Roll Mat Boxing". A roll mat is a rolled up, thin sheet of foam that's used for sleeping on when in the field. In the Parachute Regiment these are cut down to minimise size and the only time a full-size one is used is in the Arctic, because of the extreme-cold floor. I still have one that I've owned for over twenty years, it's cut to the right size from my shoulders to my ass and fits easily under the top flap of a bergan when folded into four. For roll mat boxing full roll mats are required, so the event will have to be planned in advance. Two soldiers are pitted against one another, and their arms are inserted into the long roll of foam, which act as padding and splints, denying them the ability to bend their arms. They then fight, swinging wildly at each other for a set period, or until one is knocked down. It's not rocket science.

One of my favourite contests was always a "Man's flick". That is the Para Reg term for a coin toss, but you have to be man enough to fulfil the agreed penalty if you lose. Man's flicks can be decided via heads or tails or odds and evens, where the odd one wins or loses. I think winning a man's flick is the thing that gives me the most amount of joy ever, but I also absolutely hate losing them. We used to flick for who paid for taxis, who paid for pizza, who went on duty, who drove, who carried all the weapons to the armoury, who made the brews, anything, and everything. On the extreme end there were blokes who did man's flicks for much higher stakes, such as slave for the day, chair for the day and table for the day. These were brutal, with slave for the day being the worst by far. The slave would have to do everything they were told, and the blokes would run them ragged, ironing clothes, polishing boots, cutting up food and feeding people, changing channels on the T.V, any order had to be obeyed without question and every order was delivered in a hateful manner. Slaves would even get sent to the shops with a food order and have to pay for it with their own money, it was mental. Table or chair for the day were just that, and on hearing one of the blokes shout "Table!" or "Chair!" the loser had to sprint to their location and either kneel on their hands and knees like a table, or squat, with their legs bent at 90 degrees and parallel to the floor like a chair. Tables would be used for placing plates, drinks, T.V remote controls on, or sometimes as a foot rest. Chairs were for sitting on, obviously. The only deterrent from taking it too far and totally beasting the losers was that it could be you next time.

In 3 PARA cookhouse in Dover, my Platoon had its own unofficial table that we sat at every meal time. Everyone knew it was our table and left it empty so we could all sit together on it. Some of the other Platoons like the Anti-tanks and Mortars had their own tables too. There were a few unwritten rules on those tables, the main one at ours being;

Never leave your scoff unattended!

Abandoning a plate or bowl of food to fetch a drink, or some cutlery was a basic, schoolboy error, and would result in acts of immediate skulduggery by those remaining at the table. Desserts and drinks were poured over mains, entire bottles of salt were dumped on meals and cutlery was stuffed into food, handle first. It was so childish, but really funny and everyone would just sit there, straight faced like nothing had happened when the victim returned. Another rule was;

Never leave your diggers / cutlery unattended!

Most of us only used a spoon, and your spoon had to be treated like a weapon – Always within arm's reach. Unsecured diggers were bent in half within an instant, the blokes would snatch them, bend them, and put them back folded in half the second you turned your back. Almost everyone's diggers were kinked along the shaft where they'd been sabotaged then straightened back out. Sometimes the diggers would be plastic which had a tendency to snap rather than bend, which was even funnier.

One weekend, when camp was very quiet, a few of us were sat at our usual table when we were joined by a young officer. He was new and covering as Duty Officer for the weekend but none of us knew him. As he sat, we all looked at him suspiciously, then looked at each other perplexed.

"Good afternoon gents." He said politely.

We nodded in recognition, but nobody spoke. He was not only a crow, but also an officer, and a trespasser, he must have felt really awkward by our response. A couple of seconds after sitting he stood up, and moved towards the drink dispenser a few metres away, leaving behind a full set of diggers and his scoff. Simultaneously I grabbed his fork, Scotty grabbed his knife, and Mac snatched his spoon. We bent them in half then stuffed them into his spaghetti Bolognese, submerging them in the hot meat sauce. He came back with some juice and sat back down.

"Oh!" he said, noticing his diggers. "That's odd."

We were all looking down, eating our food, and doing our best not to laugh, if we'd looked up, we'd have burst out in hysterics. One piece at a time he pulled out the cutlery and wiped it down with some napkins, wondering what the hell was going on. We ate the rest of the meal in silence and then all got up together and left while he returned to the hotplate, to get some pudding. He took his diggers with him that time but returned to an empty table.

THE PHANTOM

In the Para battalions there dwells a mysterious, insidious character, who only comes out at night, to strike at the vulnerable and defenceless as they sleep. Nameless, faceless, and shameless, he is known as **The Phantom!** As a new bloke in 3 PARA I was once mercilessly attacked by the Phantom the night before going on Leave. These nights are usually a massive party, where the whole battalion goes into town and gets hammered, and like everyone else that night, I returned from Aldershot town in a paralytic state, falling into a coma-like sleep as soon as my head hit my pillow, oblivious to everything, until I woke up several hours later. Looking in the mirror for the first time in the morning, it took me a few seconds to work out what was wrong, but something was amiss! Back then I had a full head of blonde hair, albeit very short, and my eyebrows were even blonder. Moving closer to the mirror, I quickly realised what was wrong. My eyebrows were diffy! (Deficient / Not there) The Phantom had struck. I was gutted, and now it stood out like a sore thumb, it couldn't be unseen. I asked around to see if anyone knew who'd done it but the only response I got was "The Phantom!" accompanied by laughter, and the blokes pointing at me and telling me I looked stupid. I knew that already. When I took the bin bags outside to the skip, I saw another bloke with his eyebrows missing too, a mate also called Steve. He was worse off than me though because he had dark hair, and The Phantom had not only done his eyebrows, but he'd also shaved a line down the middle of his head as well. It turned out The Phantom had been a busy boy that night, and all the victims had one thing in common, we were all Joe Crows, new blokes. I went on leave that afternoon, and got the train from Aldershot to Aylesbury, where I was going to spend time with an old girlfriend. The entire journey I was convinced that people were staring at me, and I felt like a right freak. When I got to my girlfriend's house, her older sister was there visiting, and opened the door. I knew she'd noticed my deformity straight away, I could tell by the way she looked at me, so I just got it out of the way as soon as I saw her.

"My eyebrows got shaved off last night." I explained, pointing to my face.

Turned out she hadn't noticed after all.

"What?" she said, slightly surprised by my announcement. She leaned forward to inspect, and after a couple of seconds her hand went over her mouth as she gasped. "Oh my God, you've got no eyebrows!"

It was at that point I realised that it wasn't as apparent as I thought, and maybe I should have kept my mouth shut, because she rushed off to tell everyone else in the household.

The Phantom attacked me one more time after that, but this time I woke up mid-procedure and he ran off. In my drunken state I walked into the ablutions to check the damage, and discovered one eyebrow was gone, but the other was still intact. By then I wasn't such a complete Crow anymore but had still only been in 3 PARA for about a year. I was really angry this time though, and went through the block, kicking doors open and shouting at people in their beds. I'd picked up the discarded razor and was storming around with it in my hand screaming. "Did you fucking do this to me?!" I was going to find out who it was and shave their eyebrows off. I was on a mission, and I'd kept my head down for long enough. This time I took it personally and wasn't prepared to accept it as part of some drawn out initiation process. Understandably nobody confessed, even the bloke I suspected most seemed to be asleep when I burst through his door like a raving lunatic. It was pretty clear I was prepared for violence. Eventually I calmed down and went back to bed, still feeling angry when I woke up in the morning. It was one of the blokes' last day in the army that day and that's why we'd been out for a drink. Daz, who'd been my primary suspect, had done a good few years, but decided to get out and try something else while he was still young. I said my goodbyes, shook his hand, and wished him all the best in civvy street. A few minutes later, I was sat on the toilet in the ablutions when I heard Daz's voice on the other side of the door.

"Steve?" he called.

I was surprised to hear him. "Alright Daz? I thought you'd gone mate. Have you changed your mind already?" I asked him.

Daz spoke solemnly. "I'm really sorry mate, it was me who shaved your eyebrow. I feel like a right prick for doing it. I was drunk, I'm really sorry mate." He reached his hand under the door to shake hands, and I accepted it.

"It's alright mate." I said. "It'll grow back." I really respected him for that. It obviously played on his mind, and I guess he didn't want anyone else getting the blame either. He was a good bloke.

A good mate of mine in 3 PARA called Jim didn't see the funny side when his eyebrows were shaved off once either. We were in Norway, on the Military Ski Instructor course, and when you're in extremely cold places you appreciate every hair on your head, because it helps to keep you warm. As usual beer had been involved, and Jim had woken up with two eyebrows less than what he went to sleep with. This style did not suit him at all though, and made him look very odd, because he had dark hair and pronounced eyebrow sockets. In a desperate attempt to normalise his appearance, Jim decided to shave his entire head, but he looked far from normal after that. He looked like a complete nutcase! Like a cross between Bond villain Blofeld and Don Logan, the Ben Kingsley character in "Sexy Beast." Jim thought he knew who'd done the deed, but never actually called anyone out, instead he'd make comments about revenge, and walk around with a razor in his hand or pocket. We all knew who the Phantom was on this occasion, a really popular, funny bloke called H, and he was getting increasingly anxious about the inevitable, impending counter-attack. Still without confessing to his guilt, H attempted to avoid Jim's vengeance through negotiation. They had been friends for years, but it was becoming awkward.

"Jim, I don't know who it was that done your eyebrows, but it wasn't me mate." H stated.

Jim was keeping his cards close to his chest. "Don't worry H, I know exactly who it was, and they're going to wish they'd never met me by the time I'm finished with them." he said sinisterly. "Everyone has to sleep, and when they do, I'll be there, waiting."

H was understandably worried. Day to day, Jim was one of the nicest blokes you could ever meet, but like many soldiers, he also had the ability to turn on the aggression in an instant and was slightly unpredictable.

H continued his appeal. "Just as long as you don't think it was me mate, because I had nothing to do with it." he lied.

"There's always innocent casualties in war." Jim replied earnestly. He was winning the psychological battle.

This went on for a couple of weeks as Jim kept everyone guessing. He was obviously enjoying watching people squirm, and there were several people sleeping with one eye open, because he never actually blamed anybody, he just made the odd ambiguous comment like;

"Oh is that where you sleep is it?" or "I wonder what you would look like if someone shaved off your eyebrows?" A few times there would be a bunch of us in a room, having a beer or chewing the fat, when the door would open slowly, and a disposable razor would come skating across the floor to the shout "Grenade!" from the thrower. We never saw him, but Jim's voice was unmistakeable. H was so on-edge that a few times he opted to sleep outside in the -20°C cold. He secretly locked himself into the back of the BV206 all-terrain vehicles we had outside, which is just like sleeping in a very cold fridge. In the end Jim let it go, he was only kidding, but his strategy worked much better than any physical retribution.

Another, more stealthy method of hair removal favoured by The Phantom was a hair removal cream called Imac. The Phantom would pour Imac into the shower gel bottles of their selected victims, who would then unwittingly administer the magic potion to themselves. You could always tell when someone had been sabotaged, because there would be random, indiscriminate clumps of hair missing from their heads, like they were suffering a bad case of alopecia, or they'd been attacked by a garden strimmer. Most people would just shave their heads completely afterwards if they fell prey to the Imac Phantom.

Shower gel has been the chosen delivery vehicle for other biological warfare munitions by friends of mine too. During an overseas exercise, a mate called Ted was sharing a room with an officer, who decided that Ted's shower gel was much more alluring than his own, and seemingly preferred his deodorant too, as he consistently used both. When he continued to use it after Ted had asked him not to, Ted took action, opting for a moral victory over a physical or visible punishment. For this act of retribution the selected active ingredient was Ted's very own semen, which he carefully "injected" into the bottle, then watched in quiet satisfaction, as it depleted over the next few days, while he used another bottle. Everyone knew, except the bloke who was having a one-man bukkake party every night. It was grim, but good for morale. Our morale.

ROBOCOP

Just before my posting back to the Pathfinders as the sergeant major, I went to the compound to visit some mates who were still serving there. My good friend Gaz was the Platoon Sergeant, and he asked me if I wanted to introduce myself to the blokes. There were only about twenty of them there at the time, but because it's such a busy unit, that was a good number of people to capture in one go, so I did it.

I'd been away at other jobs for five years, so there were lots of new faces to me. I told them who I was, how pleased I was to be returning to the Pathfinders, and what they should expect from me as their sergeant major. In retrospect it might have come across as very cliché, but I was probably aware of that risk, but hoped they'd realise I was actually sincere. I told them that I would work hard for them, that I'd protect them and the Pathfinder's reputation, that I expected them to work hard for me, that I didn't like bullshit, and I would always be up front and honest with them. With that I expected the same from them, and they should never be afraid to tell me the truth, whatever they'd done they could tell me, and know that I would always be fair. Firm but fair. Well aware that I look like a miserable old bastard I reassured them. "Despite how I might look, I am approachable, and my door is always open." I said. "Unless it's shut. And if it's shut, come back later."

I though it went well enough.

A few weeks later I arrived at the compound to start my tenure as the Sergeant Major, and on day-one while I was getting myself a brew, I had a look at the notice board in the small kitchen area while the kettle boiled. This board was more a space for the blokes to anonymously abuse each other rather than display meaningful information and was always good for a laugh. Drawings, photographs, and magazine articles relating to individuals in a defamatory manner filled the board, with a few that were still there from five years before. Among them was a picture of the 1980's movie character Robocop with the words "I am approachable. My door is always open." In a speech bubble from his mouth. At the bottom of the picture was the title PF Sergeant Major. I collared one of the blokes, a Zimbabwean called Dave and asked him. "What's that all about mate?" I've been likened to a few characters before, usually Jason Statham or The Kurgan from the original Highlander movie, and struggled to see a resemblance, but Robocop was a first.

Dave feigned ignorance. "I don't know Steve. It's probably because you are like the new sheriff in town or something like that." he said. He knew exactly what it meant but didn't want to be the one to explain it to the old man. I had no idea that "Robocop" had become a well-used term for calling out blatant untruths. As punishment for getting caught lying, the blokes were getting the front half of their heads shaved bald in an ingenious way of humiliating them, whilst also letting everyone else know that they'd been bullshitting. Some people even shaved their own heads as an admission of guilt for crimes such as; lying about the attractiveness of a girl they pulled or choosing to go on a date with their girlfriend over a night out with the blokes.

I found out who put that poster up, but never let the bloke know that I knew. He was a mega bloke, and we trained martial arts together quite a few times. I wound him up on a couple of occasions, asking him if he knew who'd made the poster, because I was going to get some revenge. Yes Hodgy, I knew it was you all along! Good skills mate.

"My door is always open. I am approachable."

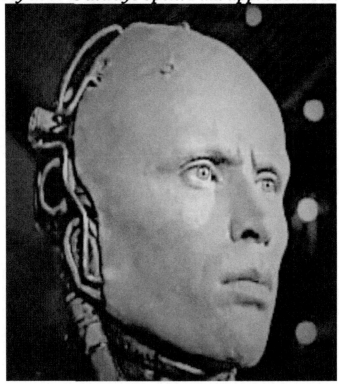

Pathfinders Sergeant Major

EASE UP, WISE UP, LOOK OUT GEEZER, HEADBUTT!

The Kray twins must have been massive employers back in the day, second only to the NHS and maybe the Post Office in London. I say that because just about every Cockney I've ever met has told me his dad worked for them, usually as a driver or debt collector. One bloke I met was explaining to me how he could cut a thirty minute conversation down to merely a few words of Cockney rhyming slang, when talking to his father, another Cockney.

"So, for example, if I wanted to sell you a watch, what do you think I'd say to you?" he asked me.

The answer was too obvious, so I knew it would be wrong, but tried anyway. "You'd say, do you want to buy a watch?" I guessed.

"No!" he said, smirking smugly and shaking his head, like I was stupid.

I didn't actually care what the answer was, but I played along. "I give up mate, tell me."

"I'd say; Do you wanna buy a kettle!" he answered coyly, before explaining. "Because if I'm selling a watch, it's probably stolen, and if there's a copper nearby, I don't want him to know I'm selling stolen goods. So I'd say, do you wanna buy a kettle?"

I tried my best to find a rhyming connection between a watch and a kettle, but I couldn't do it, so I asked him. "But what has a kettle got to do with a watch?"

He looked really pleased with himself as he revealed the conundrum. "A watched kettle never boils!" he stated dramatically.
I was disappointed after all the build-up. "For one, that doesn't rhyme! And two, wouldn't the copper just think you were selling a stolen kettle instead?" I said.
Imagine the confusion of buying something from that idiot!

As a teenager I dated a girl from West London. She lived with her parents, and I used to go there at the weekend. The house was always busy with people buying and selling stolen property like meat, booze, cigarettes, clothing, and perfume. Drugs were also sold there and there always seemed to be someone shouting. Often when talking about fights or violence somebody would say something like "Yeah, that's what it's like in London!" These comments were obviously for my benefit, I was the non-Londoner who knew nothing about hostility. One day, I was sat in the living room and there were a few shady characters visiting, obviously up to no good. Two of the young men started arguing, and one of them, a skinny bloke in a leather jacket and tracksuit trousers, got up and went through the door to the adjoining kitchen. The remaining man continued to berate the other who could obviously hear him through the flimsy door, and suddenly that door burst open. Stood in the open doorway the man in the leather jacket pointed to the other menacingly and shouted:
"Ease up, wise up, look out Geezer, head butt!" He said it very fast and straight faced.
I started laughing, I thought it was a joke, but realised he might be serious when he stood there with his chest puffed out and arms wide, like he was carrying invisible carpets. After a short pause in that pose and terrifying stare down, he stepped back into the kitchen and closed the door once more.
Seemingly I was the only person in the room who thought that was a strange event because nobody else was laughing, everyone had gone quiet.
I turned to a bloke sat next to me. "What did he just say?" I asked.
He replied as fluently as the first man had said it. "Ease up, wise

up, look out Geezer, head butt!" he repeated.

I asked him to say it a couple more times so I could commit it to memory.

"Is that some sort of threat?" I queried. "Or was that a joke?"

"It means shut your mouth or I'm gonna stick the nut on you. He was warning him." I was informed.

I couldn't believe it, where I was from that was fighting talk and would have been dealt with there and then, but this was a much funnier conclusion.

Two German Shepherd dogs also lived at that house, and they were as nuts as everyone else. I always get on with dogs and they liked me, but if they didn't like someone they'd be secured in another part of the house to stop them attacking. You could hear them going mental, barking, and banging against doors and walls when people they didn't like were in the house. One evening I was asked to take both dogs for a walk, so I grabbed their extending leads and took them outside. It was quite late and dark, but the street lights lit up the large green near the house well enough, so I went there. I kept them both on their leads because of their unpredictability and was only alerted to the presence of another person by the sudden direction change and increase of speed by both dogs. I looked up to see the shadowy figure of a man walking across the field at the opposite end, and realised the dogs were running towards him. The extendable leads were paying out rapidly, making a whirring sound as the dogs accelerated, and I pushed the button on them both to lock them in place, leaning back and bracing myself in preparation for the jolt. I called the dogs names, but they weren't listening, they had target fixation.

"Fucking run mate!" I shouted. I wasn't confident in the durability of those leads.

"Fucking run!" I yelled again. The leads went taught, yanking me forwards and I alternated between skidding along the wet grass like a water skier, and running behind those crazy dogs. Luckily, the man recognised the perilous situation he was in and sprinted to a nearby fence, jumping over it and disappearing safely. That could have ended really badly for all of us.

Another time I took one of the dogs for a walk was while visiting my ex-girlfriend in her flat. A mate of mine called Dan had come to see me one night, and we decided to go and get a few beers from the local off licence. She asked me to take the dog, and seeing as though she lived in a small, ninth-floor flat, and hardly ever took it out herself, I thought it was a good idea. The lift was only small, with the usual scent of urine and scruffy graffiti on the walls you'd expect from a London block of flats. With my friend and I, plus the German Shepherd there wasn't that much space when it stopped on the fifth floor on the way down. The dented door screeched open, and a man went to step inside, quickly changing his mind and jumping backwards when the dog snapped at him with a high pitched bark. Luckily, I had her on a short lead and managed to pull her back in time, but he made the right decision to get out, that dog was nasty. The door closed again as I told the dog off, giving it a tap on the nose and talking sternly. "Bad dog!" I said. She growled at me and showed her teeth, and suddenly the lift seemed a whole lot smaller, if she attacked me there was nowhere to go. I stood my ground. "Rosie, sit!" I ordered firmly. Thankfully, she sat obediently, and we were back on track. Stepping outside there was nobody around, so I let the dog off its lead, immediately regretting it when a much smaller dog walked around the corner right in front of us, closely followed by its owner. Rosie ran straight across the paved forecourt and picked up the tiny animal in her mouth as the other owner starting shouting worriedly. I ran over to Rosie and grabbed her by the collar shouting "Drop it!"
At the exact moment that I bent down the other man swung a punch towards the back of my head, missing as I ducked. I only found out afterwards because my friend had seen it and told me. Rosie released the dog and as I stood upright a second punch connected with the back of my skull. I let go of Rosie and turned around to face my attacker who was obviously furious.

"Who the fuck do you think you're hitting?" I said. I wasn't even angry, more disappointed that I'd tried to help, and he'd failed to see that. He cocked his hand to throw another punch and I instinctively delivered a low kick to his lead leg to throw him off balance, followed by a leading right hand to the chin before my foot even touched the floor. He stumbled backwards and fell into a wall behind him, so I followed up with a couple of knees as he covered up in a crouching position. I remember I still wasn't angry, just doing what was right, defending myself. He was protecting his face well, and I foolishly punched him on the top of his head, breaking my hand in the process. When he started screaming his apologies, my friend intervened.

"Leave him Steve, he's had enough mate." Dan said.

I stepped back and let him get up. I understood he was frightened for his dogs safety, but he shouldn't have attacked me. I gave him a piece of my mind and we parted ways. Dan had got control of Rosie while I debriefed him and I don't know if his dog was dead, but as he walked off carrying it in his arms, it wasn't moving. When we returned to the flat I told my ex-girlfriend what had happened; that her dog had attacked a person and possibly killed another dog, and that I'd been in a fight and broken my hand punching someone in the head. She didn't give a monkey's. That relationship ended soon afterwards. ·

CHAPTER SIX

Allegedly Rumoured

THE PENCIL IS MIGHTIER THAN THE SWORD

When I was about ten years old I went on a field trip with my middle school to some kind of manor in the countryside. It was the first time I'd done anything like that because we could never afford that kind of thing before my mum married my stepdad. During the day we learned about the local flora and fauna and conducted experiments, usually in pairs. I was partnered up with a kid called Johnathan for one task, where we had to count the different bugs and plants within a designated area, record the findings and produce a table of results. Johnathan was the tall, lanky kid in class, towering above the rest of us, and we usually got on well. For the experiment we agreed that I would do the searching and counting, and he would do the recording in his notebook, and together we gathered a lot of data. However, when we finished and I asked him to show me the numbers he refused, saying it was his work and I should do my own. He was kneeling down on the grass, and when I got aggressive and tried to snatch away his book, he back-handed my leg angrily. In response I punched him in the face hard, causing him to fall on the ground, crying loudly. When he sat up, I was surprised to see a fair amount of blood running down his face from a cut below his eye. I looked at my clenched fist and realised that I was still holding my pencil, the tip broken off. As he rolled around screaming a teacher rushed over and was shocked to see the blood. I realised that I'd inadvertently stabbed him in the face with the pencil and quickly discarded it into the tall grass.

"Give me the ring!" the teacher demanded, holding out his hand to me.

"What ring?" I asked.

"You must be wearing a ring to cause a cut like that!" he said sternly. "Hand it over now!"

There was no way I was going to admit that I'd actually just stabbed someone with an HB2, standard issue school pencil, so I kept my mouth shut. I was actually worried he'd get lead poisoning and I'd be found out, but he was alright.

JOHNNY DOE

In the parachute battalions' sergeants' and officers' messes, before civilians were brought in, the jobs of mess manager and mess steward were done by the soldiers. The mess manager was a sergeant and supporting him would be a corporal and a couple of privates. Not the most sought after jobs, they were usually given to soldiers as either a punishment posting, somewhere to recover from injury, or a last job for someone being discharged from service. A couple of good friends of mine were posted to the Mess during their time, against their will. The first, Johnny D, lasted one day before he was sent back to his company. An extremely fit paratrooper, Johnny was well known for his boxing skills and his infectious sense of humour, but when he was sent to the Warrant Officer's and Sergeant's Mess, his humour failed him. On his first day, during lunch time, he was briefed by the Mess Sergeant how to serve the soldiers who were sat at the grand wooden table in the dining room. He listened intently to how he should carry in a large bowl of chips, which route to take, and where to place it so they could help themselves. When the brief was finished, he picked up the bowl and carried it to the large double-doors, where he paused momentarily and took a deep breath. Then, as hard as he could, he kicked that door, bursting it open with a violent bang as it swung out on its hinges. The diners turned quickly in their seats as Johnny stormed in with the bowl and screamed at the top of his voice. "Who wants fucking chiiiiiiips!!??"
One of the sergeant majors looked at him in disbelief. "Get that man out of this mess now!" he ordered.
Johnny was posted back to his old company with immediate

effect, and never worked in the mess again.

My favourite story that circulated about Johnny was that he'd once kidnapped a man and held him captive in our barracks. In the mid-to-late 1990's the ferries that ran from Dover to Calais drew a large amount of undesirables, because of the cheap tobacco and alcohol products available onboard. For £2 you could get a return ticket, and with that, a duty-free voucher. Products were so cheap, that you would easily double your money and extra duty free vouchers were readily available from touts once you set sail. A box of two hundred cigarettes would cost £10 and quickly sell for £20 in any of the local pubs in Dover, or £25 if you tried a bit harder. At the risk of excess contraband being confiscated if caught at customs, people would buy thousands of cigarettes and gallons of spirits, making as many cross-channel trips as they could in a day. As long as you walked down the gangplank and touched the ground in Calais, you were allowed straight back on, to return immediately to Dover, they even had a man at the bottom of the walkway for you to walk around. For a while there was an influx of men from the north-west, especially Liverpool into our adopted town, who stayed in local bed & breakfasts for a week at a time, loading up with duty frees during the day, and getting into fights with us at night.

One afternoon during a weekend off, Johnny and another 3 PARA bloke called Mark decided to pop over to France for something to do. The plan was to have a few beers on board, stock up on booze for the next couple of weeks, then hit the pubs when they got back that evening. After a few hours, they were stood out on deck, heading back into Dover, having bought their allowances on the outward and return legs. Passing through the high walls of the harbour they were approached by a loud, drunk scouser who barged into their conversation and draped his arms over their shoulders like they were old friends.
"Gizza fag lad." He asked rudely, looking at Johnny.
Mark answered for them both. "We don't smoke mate." He stated

bluntly.

The scouser looked down at the duty free carrier bags by their feet. Inside one of them the tops of two boxes of Embassy No1 cigarettes were clearly visible.

"Don't be a twat mate, you either give me one, or I fucking knock you out and take two hundred!" the stranger threatened, standing up straight to deliver his reply.

Johnny gave fair warning. "Fuck off before you get yourself hurt! I won't tell you again!"

Acknowledging the intent in Johnny's voice, and the impressiveness of Marks massive physique, the man decided to conduct a tactical withdrawal, but as he left issued a menacing threat to the two paratroopers.

"We'll see who gets hurt, when we're off this ferry, and me and my mates cut you to fucking ribbons!" he warned, taking a mobile phone from his pocket.

Experience told them that he would be calling for reinforcements, because that had happened before on several occasions during fights in the town, where knives had been used too.

Without saying a word to each other, Johnny and Mark ran towards him, grabbed an arm and a grip of his waist band each, dragged him to the side of the ship, and threw him overboard into the sea. It was a long way down to the cold water, and the two soldiers laughed as he struck it hard, making a small splash amongst the waves caused by the slow-moving ferry as it came in to dock.

Clearing customs quickly, Johnny and Mark took a diversion and walked to the harbour wall, walking along it until they came to a ladder that went down to the water where they stopped and crouched. It was dark now, but the lights from the port illuminated the water enough for them to see their target, swimming towards another ladder further along. Reaching the ladder he paused, holding on and gasping for air after his exhausting swim fully clothed. Gaining his composure he climbed the ladder, but his relief rapidly turned to shock when he was grabbed by the two men and hauled onto the hard ground.

"Hello mate!" they said menacingly, picking him up and dragging him back along the wall to the taxi rank outside the passenger terminal. Opening the door and getting in first Johnny sat in the back seat of the cab and Mark bundled in their companion before getting in himself, wedging the terrified scouser between them, screaming for help.

Turning around in his seat, the driver demanded to know what was going on.

"They're fucking kidnapping me! The bastards tried to kill me!" shouted the captive.

Johnny improvised on the spot, flashing his army I.D card and declaring. "We are military police officers. This soldier has gone AWOL from the army, and we are arresting him and taking him to the barracks for processing!"

The scouser was stunned. "I'm not even in the army! They're fucking mental!" he yelled.

Mark joined in the bluff. "You went AWOL, you got caught. Now act like a man, and fucking behave yourself!" he ordered.

The driver fell for it and began the short drive to Connaught Barracks, opposite Dover Castle at the top of a steep hill.

Arriving at the front gate the taxi stopped, and the scouser saw the large sign affixed to the gate, displaying a silver cap badge and the words *"Third Battalion, The Parachute Regiment"* For some reason this heightened his anxiety even further, and he struggled violently as he was dragged from the vehicle and man-handled through the gate. The two soldiers on duty immediately recognised the potential for a drama and acted swiftly, raising the barrier so Johnny and Mark could get him in without knocking his head on it. The last thing anyone wanted was to damage the barrier! The next time that bloke was seen was a few hours later, when he sprinted back out of that gate barefooted, and turned towards town. Nobody knows what happened in between those last two sightings.

THIRD BATTALION

THE PARACHUTE REGIMENT

LIFE'S A DRAG

Overseas military exercises normally have an element of R+R planned into them for the blokes to unwind, relax, travel, and sample the local culture. Nine times out of ten though, when left to the men to choose, it will result in very little travel or culture, and a large consumption of local alcohol. A foreign exercise in 1994 was no different. We got a night off in a small town, where cheap accommodation had been organised by the Company Headquarters, and stocked up on beer from the nearest supermarket to drink by the swimming pool. Well-oiled from the cheap beer we headed into town, eventually ending up in a dodgy nightclub on it's outskirts. Inside was rudimentary and dark, with a few flashing lights, and a bloke behind a table with a single-deck record player. The bar had no drinks on tap, instead they sold slightly chilled cans of beer like the one's we'd bought earlier. The toilet was outside, and by outside I mean anywhere outside, but everyone was friendly, and the blokes were enjoying themselves, showing off the famous "Airborne Two-step" to impress the ladies.

One local man however, seemed unhappy that we were there and spent the night walking up to the blokes and staring at them. He didn't speak, he just stared, wide eyed and non-emotional. Every few minutes he'd move on to his next target, standing uncomfortably close beside them with his arms hanging loosely by his side. It wasn't an aggressive posture, but it was irritating, I think we all just assumed he was either mentally ill, or on drugs, or both. To the paras credit, everyone miraculously kept their hands in their pockets and ignored him. At the end of the night, a couple of lads who who'd volunteered to drive started picking everyone up and driving them back to the hotel, in groups of threes and fours. The last person to be targeted by the weirdo inside was my friend T, an excellent soldier that I looked up to, who was uncharacteristically tolerant to this strange man who followed him outside. By now the man's posture had changed, and he stood next to T with an outstretched hand, as if begging. Maybe that had been his intent the whole time; to get some money, but he'd blown that chance by annoying everyone.

"Fuck off!" T eventually shouted loudly, pointing into the distance.

Instead of doing that, the man began pointing into his outstretched hand with the other one, and his expression turned angry, frowning hard and clenching his jaw tight.

"Fuck...Off...You...Twat!" T tried again, but the bloke was having none of it and stood his ground, staring into T's eyes intently.

Just then one of the cars returned and we were next in line. Another friend called Lee was also waiting with us, and he opened the back door, got in, and shuffled across to the middle of the back seat. I got in after him, and T walked around to the other side, closely followed by his new, best buddy. Someone else was getting in the front passenger seat as T sat down and closed the door. The local was still standing with his hand out, and T beckoned him forwards. "Alright, alright, I'll give you something. Here you go mate. Give me your hand." he said, implying he was going to give some money away. The beggar extended his hand through the open window and T grabbed his arm quickly, with both hands.

"Drive Pete! Drive!" he shouted urgently to our driver, who accelerated quickly from a standing start, unsure what was happening. The bloke was now facing backwards and running to keep up, but his expression didn't change at all, maintaining his stare at T the whole time. He was impressively fast at running backwards but disappeared after the second gear change, as he fell and got dragged alongside the car.

"For fucks sake T, let him go!" Lee shouted.

T released his grip and put his hands up. "Alright!" he said.

We turned around to look through the rear window and could just make out the silhouette of the man as he stopped rolling down the dirt track and got to his feet.

The next morning we were woken up and told to get into the courtyard for a brief from one of the sergeants also staying at the hotel.

"Right, be quiet! Listen in!" he said, starting abruptly. It was obviously going to be a bollocking. "I have just spent the last hour talking to a man, who claims one of you fucking lunatics, dragged him down a road, beside a car, and left him for dead in the fucking gutter! he explained. He didn't seem angry, more fed up. As the senior rank, he'd been summoned by the hotel staff at the victim's request. He continued. "Judging by the state of his clothes, and the cuts and bruises all over his body, I have a sneaking suspicion that he's telling the truth!"

I quickly looked across to Lee, who was looking at me too. We weren't going to say anything. The sergeant went on to tell us that the man had demanded money, or else he was going to the police, and that the bribe had been paid from his own pocket. There was no way of telling if the police would still get told, but he wanted his money back, and told us what room he was in so the guilty person could pay him discretely. T owned up and paid him. I think it worked out to about £40 and nothing more was ever heard about it.

MESSY MESSES

Before it was contracted out to civilians, waitering duty in the Sergeants' and Officers' Mess functions was done by the Private soldiers from the battalions. I only ever did it twice, once in Depot, and once in Aldershot. I absolutely hated it, we were paratroopers, not waiters. I thought it was an insult to my cap badge, degrading. Everyone had had to do it, but that didn't make it right. To me, paratroopers were like vicious dogs on a short leash, barely under control, and poised to attack at any moment. Laying tables, and serving food and drinks was not something you'd expect them to excel at. I wasn't the only one who did it begrudgingly, the discontent among us was obvious and the forced politeness was blatant. It wasn't long before the blokes starting playing up, with all that alcohol being served it was only a matter of time before we started drinking some of it. It started with blokes finishing off half-empty glasses of wine that came in to the kitchen, but quickly escalated to them just pouring their own, and with alcohol comes mischief. I don't know how the officers or sergeants could eat or drink anything served to them by the blokes, after what I saw and heard about. Surely it was exactly the same when they'd done waitering as young soldiers. The good blokes that everyone liked were safe, and so were their partners, the blokes made sure their stuff got left alone. But the one's nobody liked or bore a grudge against, they got properly stitched up, and their partners were guilty by association, so they got it too.

Like everything else, the sabotage escalated as well. It started off with fairly tame antics, like someone licking a spoon, or spitting into some soup. but the further into the service we went, and the more alcohol was drank, the worse / better it got. All sorts of things were getting added to the menu; pubic hairs, bogeys, snot, and phlegm were being consumed by many unsuspecting diners. Food was getting rubbed in armpits, ass cracks, ball sacks and the floor, and I even saw a bloke climb on top of a table to urinate into the drinks dispenser. It was grim, but really, really funny. Revenge was literally a dish served cold, and hot. After that night I paid someone else to do my duty for me every other time, and went down town instead.

THE WORLD'S OLDEST PROFESSION

Las Vegas is a great place to visit, and thanks to the military I've been fortunate to go there many times. At night you can see it from miles away, as the bright lights glow like a beacon in the middle of the barren Nevada desert. "The Strip" is the four mile stretch of Las Vegas Boulevard where all the action happens. Lined with famous hotels, casinos, attractions, souvenir shops, restaurants, and bars, it's a perpetual back and forth exchange of people, traffic, and money. Activities that are illegal in most places on earth are perfectly legal there, and the first time you walk through a small cloud of exhaled marijuana smoke or see a large van drive past advertising "Call girls, direct to you in 20 minutes" it's quite a culture shock. Dozens of middle aged men and women stand at the edge of sidewalks passing out business cards for escort agencies, and the inherent politeness of the British means you end up with a pocket full of them by the end of your first night. For the married man, this unwanted collection of smut could look very suspicious to their partner on returning home, so it is discarded with some urgency. By the second night you learn to ignore them completely as they stand there trying to get your attention, make eye contact, and hand you the incriminating calling cards.

Two friends of mine, Rob, and Ken were sharing a room in a Las Vegas hotel, when curiosity got the better of one of them as he emptied his pockets and pulled out an escort agency card. Using the hotel telephone, Rob called the number printed on the front of it but hung up quickly when a ladies voice asked how she could help. He didn't actually want a hooker, he was a happily married man. He was just inquisitive about how it worked and entertaining himself while he waited for Ken to finish in the shower. A few minutes later they'd swapped places and Rob was now showering when there was a knock at the door. Ken answered it, opening the door wearing just a towel around his waist. In the corridor was a woman dressed in high heels, a short skirt, and a revealing top.

"Hello." said Ken, immediately assuming she'd got the wrong room.

The woman looked him up and down. "Hi, I'm from the agency you called. You wanna have some fun?"

Ken still thought she had the wrong room. "Sorry love, but we never called an agency." he told her.

The woman checked a message on her phone, then pointed to the number on the door. "Room 234. You definitely called!"

Rob suddenly piped up from the back of the room. "That was me. Sorry. I dialled the wrong number."

The woman tried to convince them to let her in, and got angry when they declined, accusing them of wasting her time and costing her money, so they gave her $20 for her trouble, and sent her away. Seemingly the hotel was directly linked to the agency, and caller I.D automatically informed them where Rob's call had come from.

Two different friends of mine had another interesting visit from Vegas call girls once. I was returning to my hotel room after getting breakfast, when I saw a group of soldiers huddled together with some hotel security guards, laughing loudly. I walked over to find them at a desk watching a recording from the CCTV. The guard was scrolling through footage from several different cameras, taken the previous night. The first video showed my mates entering the lobby with a couple of women who were dressed like cheap hookers. Another camera captured them in the elevator, where they got a bit frisky, and a corridor camera caught them entering the room. Fast forward an hour, and the same cameras, in reverse order, show the two rather undesirable women as they hurriedly exited the room, went down in the elevator, and out through the lobby. The earlier laughter had been caused by a very clear snapshot of the women as they looked directly at the camera. My god they were rough! Even they must have realised they were punching well above their weight with two young, fit soldiers. They still robbed them though, taking both of their wallets, but luckily not their passports, because we flew back to the UK that day.

The majority of my military freefall course was in Yuma, Arizona, and during the downtime of that course I was lucky enough to do some travelling. I went to Las Vegas, San Diego, and even got a night out in Mexico. I'd been to Cancun the previous year, so I had a little bit of an expectation, but Mexicali was a different place altogether. We'd parked our hire vehicle at a hostel on the U.S side and took taxis, so we could all have a drink and not risk the vehicle being stolen. The short drive to the city had me on edge from the get-go, with our driver taking a scenic route through some ghettos to increase the fare. It was like a budget horror film where the kids get a lift from a stranger, who is obviously going the wrong way, and kidnaps them. We were definitely driving around in circles for a while, but eventually emerged from the shady slums and arrived in the well-lit busy streets of Mexicali City. As per usual, we got hammered on beer, tequila, and whatever else was put in front of us by the enthusiastic bartenders. One of my mates was a young, single soldier and he was especially keen on drinking shots of tequila that were being dispensed from the cleavage of a petite waitress in a low-cut t-shirt. Noticing his interest, she asked him if he wanted to join her in a private booth for some sexy time and he quickly disappeared. The booths were along one side of the bar, and each had a curtain that was pulled closed when they were "busy." My friend entered one with the girl and she drew the curtain shut behind them. Ten minutes later he was standing back with us, looking surprisingly unimpressed. In the booth, for a bargain price of $20 the young lady had performed fellatio on him, and he'd enjoyed it very much, but in hindsight he was not only concerned that she hadn't used a condom, but he was also horrified by the fact that his ejaculate had been spat into a bucket that was pulled from underneath his seat when the deed was done. In that bucket, he saw a generous amount of evidence that he wasn't the first customer of the night! Classy.

PROJECTILE LAUGHING

When we were young men in 3 PARA we didn't go out to enjoy a pint; we went out to drink as many pints as possible, in the shortest time possible. Our choice of beer was based entirely on the alcohol content; the stronger the better. One night, one of my mates called Shaun was struggling to keep up with the pace as we drank about four pints an hour. We were in Dover, in a pub called The Lord Nelson, and were waiting for Shaun to finish his pint of lager so we could move on to the next pub on our well-trodden route, The Castle. He had half a pint left, and tried to leave without finishing it, putting it down on the table and gesturing towards the door. Everyone was disgusted, that was not allowed! We shook our heads and pointed to the glass.

"Drink it!" we said.

Shaun was bloated but the pressure got to him, he knew the rules. He picked up the glass and necked the rest in one go, struggling to force it into his already full stomach. As soon as his empty glass went down, we all turned towards the door to leave, but Shaun was in a real hurry to get outside and pushed his way to the front, clearly about to throw up. He got to the door first, covering his mouth with one hand, and yanking the door open with the other. We were all laughing at his obvious distress as he fought to stop himself throwing up. On the other side of the door heading into the pub was a young couple, the pretty girl made-up nicely and dressed immaculately in a red dress. It was unfortunate timing. Shaun projectile vomited that last pint directly into the face and hair of that young woman, as it sprayed out in jets between his fingers. It was strange, because he was laughing as he was retching and ran past her to puke into the gutter. We were all right behind him and were laughing too. The couple stood there in shock for a few seconds then turned around and left. Their night was over, but ours had just begun.

HOW TO MAKE A CRAPPY CUP OF TEA

Officers in the Army are normally either loved, hated, or treated with indifference by the blokes. The arrogant, condescending, snobby, self-serving, lazy, or hypocritical are loathed by their men, who don't respect them, and perform their duties begrudgingly to the minimum standard when tasked by them. These officers are reliant on their rank or their influence in the Messes and without it they are insignificant.

The timid, uncommitted, compliant, awkward, unconfident, or mediocre are treated with apathy. Soldiers will not even bother to learn their names and will blatantly walk past them without saluting or acknowledging them. Other officers will also see their weakness and step over them at the first opportunity to further their own ambitions.

The enthusiastic, fit, motivated, compassionate, aggressive, humble, and inspiring officers are respected by their men, who will work hard for them proactively without complaint. The way officers act can determine the morale of their soldiers, how well they perform, and how long they choose to stay in the service.

I worked for an officer once who was absolutely despised by everyone. He'd started his career in a different regiment, then served in Special Forces for two years, and then decided to transfer to the Parachute Regiment. It was obviously a decision based entirely on progressing his career, because he clearly detested everything about the airborne mentality. His previous unit was one of the old fashioned, pomp and ceremony type regiments, where the Officers Mess was treated like some kind of royal residence and the soldiers were looked down upon like second class citizens. Working close to him as his radio operator I regularly listened to him talking to other officers, and I hated the way he talked about the blokes like they were such a burden that spoiled his plans and made his life difficult. He had no respect for anybody, placing himself on a pedestal high above the rest of us inept imbeciles.

Parachute Regiment officers usually know better than to treat their men with contempt, because from day one in Battalion they are taken under the wing and guided through their careers by strong Senior Non-Commissioned Officers. Sergeants teach them how to run a Platoon, Sergeant Majors keep them on-track when they command a Company, and the Regimental Sergeant Major is their sounding board when they command a Battalion. This particular officer though, he'd not been handled correctly, a good old-fashioned throat chop or fish hook in his Lieutenant years might have done the job, but that time had long since passed. He had been left unsupervised, and he was now a Major, and a well-established prick, beyond repair.

One day he tried to hand me an empty mug. "Put a brew in there!" he ordered arrogantly. We were riding in the front cab of a BV206 over-snow vehicle in Norway and I was sat behind him, next to the electric boiling vessel that we'd keep topped up with snow to make brews with. Bad manners is something I've never been able to tolerate, my mum would never stand for it when I was a kid, and I was the same.
"I haven't got a brew Sir!" I said, matching his arrogance.
"Well do you want to put one on then?" he replied, still holding his mug out for me to take from him.
"No thanks, I'm not thirsty." I answered bluntly. I didn't care about him, I hated him. He was snob, and in my eyes, not even Para Reg. I was a Private soldier, a Tom, what was he going to do anyway?"

One of the other soldiers, a Lance Corporal called John, took the mug. "I'll get the brews on Sir." He offered unexpectedly.

John was a friend of mine, a mad Geordie who had been in the same platoon as me, before moving across to work in the Medical Centre as a Battalion Medic. He looked at me and nodded with a knowing wink and devious grin. As promised, he made a brew with the issued tea, whitener, and sugar from the ration pack, but added an extra ingredient before returning the mug. Inside the BV206 is very loud because the passengers sit right next to the engine, with only a fibreglass covering between them to shield the noise of the screaming diesel motor. However, when John snorted loudly, then hocked up the phlegm in his throat, I was convinced the officer would hear him. He spat into the cup and passed it forward to the obviously unaware front passenger, who took it without saying thanks, and slowly drank it all. After that, John took on the role of brew maker every time that mug was passed back but didn't spit in it every time. Instead, he put laxatives from his medical kit into it, opening up the capsules and pouring in the powder discretely.

The first day of this, the wagon came to a sudden halt on a few occasions, so the officer could run off into a bit of cover and urgently relieve himself, and that evening he visited John to see if he had anything to cure his diarrhoea. John was ready and waiting with some Imodium, anti-diarrhoeal capsules he'd already set aside when the patient arrived at our tent. I'd seen John earlier in the night, carefully pouring small amounts of powder from one tiny capsule into another and asked what he was up to. Smiling broadly, he explained how he'd been spiking the officers brews with laxatives, and was expecting him to visit, asking for Imodium. John took his time, firstly emptying the Imodium capsules, then gently opening the laxative capsules, and transferring the powder into the empty Imodium shells before studiously putting them back together again. When the visitor arrived John asked all the right questions and prescribed the "Imodium."

"Take two now, and one more after each loose stool." He advised sincerely.

Over the next couple of days that officer must have lost a stone in weight, but despite Johns best efforts he was still full of shit!

IT WASN'T ME

The accommodation at the Naval Air Facility in El Centro, California, where we used to conduct freefall training in the Pathfinders, was awesome. The rooms were like a hotel, with two large beds, cable T.V, a fridge, brew kit, and a Jack n' Jill bathroom that you shared with the room next door. As a sergeant, I was allocated my own room, and was fast asleep when there was a knock at the door one morning. Feeling a bit hung over from the previous night I got up to answer it, and was confronted by two, clearly agitated PJI's.

"There's been an incident Steve." I was informed. "One of your blokes has destroyed the toilet in the Conference Room downstairs, and the Americans are going mental!" they said.

"How do you know it's one of my blokes?" I asked defensively.

"Because there's a massive trail of evidence that goes from the toilet, all the way to his room." They replied.

That morning the cleaners had found the communal toilet in the Conference Room in a terrible state. Excrement was smeared all over the walls, door, floor, and sink, and footprints of someone who'd obviously trodden in the mess barefooted, led away from the scene. Sure enough, those footprints, although fading with each step, went directly to a room that was occupied by two of my blokes. The evidence was incriminating to say the least. The RAF guys left me alone to deal with it and I knocked on the door. The stench inside was disgusting, and the footprints continued right up to one of the beds, which had been stripped of its sheets. The occupant of the bed was busy cleaning up.

"What the fuck have you done you silly bastard?" I asked him.

He already knew he'd been accused of trashing the place. "I had nothing to do with that toilet downstairs." he told me. "I admit that I've shit the bed while I was asleep, but I didn't make that mess down there. That was someone else!"

I was surprised to hear him profess his innocence. "There's footprints from down there, all the way to your bed mate." I said. "The evidence suggests it was you."

He was adamant that it wasn't him, that he'd somehow trodden in the mess by accident, walked back to his room, then fallen asleep and shit the bed. I wasn't convinced, but he was a mate, and there was a small chance he was telling the truth.

"I'm going to ask you one more time mate, and I want you to be honest, because I've got your back either way, and I'll fight your corner. Was it you?"

"It wasn't me Steve, I swear it." he said.

I knew how it looked, but as a mate, all I could do was trust him, and as a sergeant it was my duty to defend my blokes.

By the time I met with the people in charge to tell them it wasn't us, another incident had been reported, with another one of my blokes in the frame again. This time it was about a hire car that had been wrapped up in Black Nasty tape. The car belonged to some RAF personnel, and on discovering it, they'd hastily pulled it off, taking some of the paintwork with it. Before investigating that, I let everyone know that the toilet horror scene had nothing to do with my blokes and to start looking elsewhere. I fell out with some people I'd known for a long time over that, and never felt confident that I hadn't been lied to, but without 100% proof I was always going to stick up for the blokes.

The man accused of vandalising the car was Ronnie, who'd also been drinking heavily the night before. He was a good bloke from 3 PARA, reliable and honest. I had the same conversation with him, giving him the opportunity to come clean if he was guilty. He denied it too, and I believed him. There were a few other people I suspected of that prank-gone-wrong, so I paid them a visit to see what they had to say. I was fed up with my blokes getting the blame for everything. They were pretty convincing too to be fair and in the end, both incidents were cleaned up and fixed without anyone getting disciplined. About two years after that trip I was told that it was indeed Ronnie who taped up the car, and he'd lied because he thought he'd be thrown out of the Pathfinders if he owned up. He was probably right. Sadly, Ronnie died in 2016 after falling from a hotel roof in Vietnam. Shortly before his death he'd sought help from a mental health organisation but was placed on a four month waiting list for a psychiatric assessment. RIP mate.

CHAPTER SEVEN

International Relations

WINNING HEARTS AND MINDS

In 2002 we were deployed to Kabul, Afghanistan where we worked mainly in six-man and twelve-man teams, venturing into different areas to establish which tribe, militia, or faction they were controlled by. The U.S invasion to oust the Taliban had scattered the numerous armed groups across the country and several warlords, generals and politicians claimed to be in command of tens of thousands of fighting men. Kabul had been wrecked by the fighting there, parts of it looked like a scene from the Blitz of World War Two. Large urban areas had been reduced to rubble and ruin, and unstable, partially collapsed buildings stood precariously next to roads, waiting to fall at any minute. Roads were peppered with small craters from mortar bombs and artillery shells, and it wasn't unusual to see unexploded rounds sticking out of the ground where they'd fell. It was a very complex situation that required careful handling and a large part of our job was to liaise between the Afghans themselves and build relationships between the Afghans and the coalition. One morning during our brief we were reminded about the importance of being respectful and courteous to the locals. A message had come down from up-high about winning hearts and minds to get them on side.

Later that day, we drove out to a compound just outside the city to meet with a warlord, who claimed to have a force of ten thousand fighters at his disposal. Our patrol commander entered the building with one of our blokes as close protection, and the remainder of us secured the area outside. Within a few minutes one of the Afghan security detail sauntered over to the vehicle I was sat in with my mate Bry. AK47 slung behind his back he leaned against the Land Rover.

"Hello." He said.

"Hello mate. How are you doing?" I replied.

"Very good my friend. How are you?"

"I'm very good as well, thank you."

He stared at me intently. "Do you like it here?" he asked.

Thinking about our earlier brief I answered diplomatically. "Yes of course. Afghanistan is a beautiful country. I like it very much." I said, pointing beyond a nearby obliterated group of compounds, and snapped-in-half telegraph poles to some snow covered mountains in the far distance.

He nodded in agreement. "Yes of course. We are good people here, strong people." He said proudly.

"Afghans are warriors. You beat the Soviet Army, you should be proud mate." I said.

He nodded again, seemingly happy with my appraisal, then walked around the vehicle to speak to Bry.

"Do you like Afghanistan?" he asked him.

Bry's response was blunt and to the point. "No!" he replied.

Our new friend was surprised. "Why you no like Afghanistan?" he queried.

Bry wasn't playing the game that day and chuckled as he shrugged his shoulders. "Cos it's a shit hole!" he stated honestly. "Look at it!"

There are undoubtedly some beautiful places in Afghanistan but at that time, in that place, Bry was spot on. You certainly wouldn't go there on holiday! The man walked away disappointedly, maybe nobody had brought it to his attention before.

"Erm, reference the brief about winning hearts and minds Bry..." I laughed.

"But it is a shit hole." He repeated.

"I know." I agreed.

Not restricting himself to winding up just the British, my mate Ginge proved equally proficient in foreign countries too. In Macedonia in 2001 we were conducting high level liaison tasks between the opposing forces in the conflict there. Each patrol had an interpreter embedded with them which was invaluable, not only for their translating skills, but also for their local knowledge of the area and it's customs. Most of the blokes in my team made an effort to learn some colloquial language, in an effort to endear ourselves to the people in the towns and villages we visited. We learned the basics such as yes, no, please, thank you, hello, goodbye, and a few phrases to state that we were friendly, and were there to help at the request of their government etc. Building rapport was key to gaining their confidence and trust. Some of the locals hated us though, they thought we were there to interfere or support their enemies. Not only did they hate us, but they also detested our interpreters, verbally abusing and threatening them whenever we drove or walked past. Ginge quickly lost interest in being friendly to these people, especially when he had a young girl working in his team who got very upset after some men spoke to her in their language. Seeing her frightened and intimidated, he asked her what had been said, and she told him they were threatening to rape and kill her for being a traitor and a whore. The next time I saw him a few of us were exchanging stories of what we'd been up to and comparing our new language skills, at least able to recognise the words and phrases among ourselves. Ginge joined in and said a long sentence that sounded very impressive, receiving a clap from one of the interpreters nearby in appreciation for his elocution. We were intrigued, he seemed way more advanced than any of us. "What does that mean?" I asked him.

Ginge responded with a devious grin, then chuckled. "It means, your mum's a whore, your sister fucks dogs, and your dad sucks dicks!"

I covered my face with my hands and shook my head disapprovingly. He was only saying what the rest of us were thinking, but we were supposed to be brokering peace, not inciting violence. His wicked laughter was infectious though and we all enjoyed that moment.

RELUCTANT TRANSVESTITES

In 1999, many good friends of mine in 3 PARA deployed to Kosovo on Operation Agricola. I wasn't on that tour as only about half of the battalion were sent, to bolster 1 PARA numbers. The rest of us were on exercise in Belize, all trying to convince the hierarchy that we were essential to the operational effort and should be returned home immediately to deploy. The blokes who did go came back with quite a few stories, some funny, some crazy, and some shocking. Regularly, they had been used to protect vulnerable women from violent thugs and criminals. Reports of repeated abuse and rape had been passed onto the intelligence cells and our troops had been briefed. Sometimes, the blokes would hide in the apartment or house of a victim and wait for the offenders to return. At their regular time, rapists and abusers would knock on the door and brazenly waltz inside. Many of the women had given up struggling, accepting their fate, and foregoing the beating they'd get if they fought back. The soldiers would be waiting for them though, hiding behind furniture, in cupboards, or another room, then burst out aggressively once the abusers were inside. Justice was administered to those scumbags through several different methods to convince them not to do it again, but some of the alleged punishments dealt by locals or the multi-national troops were much more inventive than others, although they could easily be made up fantasies.

Some culprits were made to change into women's clothes, had

make-up hastily applied to their faces, and were then dropped off in the middle of a busy town for all to see. Some were even driven into a town or village that was in their enemies territory, and left to make their own way back. I heard a tale that one guy, a serial rapist and suspected murderer had been driven to the edge of a known minefield and made to run through it. Many more were just beaten up or arrested, or both.

THE SEA IS CHILLY
IN CHILE

Exchange visits with foreign armed forces are a great way to share knowledge, learn new skills and develop training methods. During my time as a survival instructor I was fortunate to go on several overseas exercises, including one to Chile, South America, with three other men from the SERE School. One part of the training we did there was maritime survival, and the hosts were very keen to show us how they conducted training from their base in Quintero. Juan, our Chilean liaison officer briefed us the evening before we started and explained that we would be taking a look at the life rafts they used and practicing some sea drills with their life jackets. For the last serial, they'd be tying our hands behind our backs and our feet together, then dispatching us over the side of a boat into the sea. We laughed it off, there was no way they'd throw us in the sea while restrained. That night we were all thinking the same thing; was he serious? His delivery was impassive, like it was a perfectly normal thing to say, and I believed him.

The following morning after breakfast, we went to a small harbour to see the life raft. It was part of a life raft; the floor part. Years of wear and tear had slowly reduced it to a mere platform with no canopy, no survival aids, and no inflation device. What it did have plenty of, was holes. We jumped onto it and received a lesson on what should have been there and played along, using our imaginations, it was a bit surreal. After that we jumped back onto dry land quickly before the raft sunk, then boarded a speedboat wearing our life jackets. I don't know what the criteria for the water was to make it suitable, but we bounced along the choppy sea for a long time, before the skipper found what he was looking for and stopped. Wearing shorts and t-shirts we jumped into the cold sea, which was about 6°C and inflated our life jackets. Not surprisingly the gas bottles on the life jackets were missing too, so we blew them up manually with the inflation tubes and went through the drills they had shown us on dry land. The water was really cold which made the drills more realistic as we tried to retain heat by curling up tightly in a foetal position and holding on to each other in various configurations. At first it was funny; watching your mates suffer is always good for morale, but my sense of humour started to fail when I realised my life preserver was going down quite rapidly, and our safety boat started pulling tight turns next to us to put waves over our heads. We stopped laughing after a couple of minutes. I was shaking like a leaf and constantly blowing into the tube, with bow waves washing over my head every ten seconds. One of the other blokes called Russ realised his jacket was punctured too, which cheered me up a bit, as he now looked as stupid as me. After a while, the boat came alongside and we hauled ourselves up and over, back on deck, quickly donning the warm jackets we'd taken with us.

Heading back towards the harbour I was pleasantly surprised it was over and relieved the tied-up-drowning practice was obviously a wind-up. We entered the harbour and the boat slowed to a crawl, stopping about a hundred metres from the shore. I was right the first time, we were going over! Our host went first, explaining the exercise as rope was used to tie his hands together behind his back and his feet together at the ankles. He flopped off the side, quickly resurfaced, and swam out to his colleague on his back using a dolphin kick. Once untied he swam back to us. "Who wants to go first?" he shouted.
I was the senior rank, so I was always going to volunteer, but in this instance I hesitated and was beat to it by Gerry, an RAF sur-

vival equipment specialist and experienced windsurfer. I wasn't going to argue, I was well chuffed, who the hell wants to do that? Gerry was super-confident in the water, setting a perfect example, and against every instinct in our bodies we all followed suit. I thought I had it sussed when my turn came, I took a massive breath in to fully inflate my lungs and flopped overboard as horizontally as I could. I reckoned I wouldn't even go underwater because I'd be so buoyant. I was wrong, obviously, and under I went, probably something to do with the laws of physics. That first few seconds was pretty unnerving, but I soon resurfaced and swam the short distance to the instructor to be untied. It was a crazy thing to do, but surprisingly good, and I'd actually recommend it as a confidence building exercise.

THE EARTH MOVED

After delivering a brief to an audience of Chilean soldiers, one of my friends, who was also there congratulated me.

"Fair play mate." Gerry said. "I don't know how you kept a straight face, but good effort."

Another colleague was also impressed. "You didn't miss a beat mate. It was like nothing had even happened!" Russ added.

I had no idea what they were talking about. I thought someone in the audience must have said or done something that I'd missed. "I must have missed it gents." I confessed. "What happened?"

"The earthquake you mad bastard!" Gerry stated.

I actually missed it. I don't know how, but I did. Obviously, it was only a small one, but it got the attention of the others. I think I either assumed it was an HGV driving past, or I was distracted by the numerous blank faces in the audience, who had clearly been ordered to attend, even though they didn't speak a word of English. A colonel from the Chilean Air Force had asked me to do a presentation on the UK's Survival, Evasion, Resistance and Extraction (SERE) school where we worked. However, it quickly became obvious that he only wanted to learn about some very specific training procedures, that I was in no place to answer.

"Do you do the waterboarding technique?" he asked randomly.

"Absolutely not sir." I replied. "That is illegal. Our training is very tightly controlled and monitored."

The colonel turned to his troops and translated, receiving a few laughs and shoulder shrugs from them.

I followed up on his question. "Is that something you guys do on your course?"

He never answered that, just chuckled awkwardly before his next question.

"How do you decide when to end the interrogations of the student?" was his next query. That was quite worrying as it implied they had no strict policy on how long the exercise lasted.

He knew as well as I did that he was asking inappropriate questions about UK policy.

"Sir, I'll give you the details of the people who can answer these questions for you as I'm not involved in those decisions." I deflected. "What I can tell you, is that our students all go through exactly the same learning experience, in line with our safe system of training and MoD policy."

Again he spoke to his men in Spanish with a mixed response. Some of them seemed to like the idea of safety, others just scoffed at it, they liked their way better. I'd already been told stories of physical punishments and dangerous training methods by some of the Chileans.

"Sir." I said, wanting to clarify, deflect, and make light of the situation. "In the UK, our training is tightly governed by health and safety. For example, certain things that you might do here, would never happen within our organisation. Little things like waterboarding or throwing people into the sea while they're tied up, would be seen as a bit controversial." He got the message in the end.

VANCOUVER

After a long exercise in Wainwright, Canada, five friends and I caught a domestic flight to Vancouver to spend a few days sampling the local culture, architecture, and history (pubs). We hadn't planned or booked anything, so as soon as we arrived at Vancouver airport I grabbed a load of flyers advertising cheap accommodation in the city. My attention was quickly drawn to a backpackers hostel that charged only $7 per night and everyone agreed we should try it. Within a couple of minutes I'd called them on a payphone and booked us in for the next three nights. Outside the arrivals terminal were lots of taxis, but one of the blokes spotted a better alternative; a stretched limo. A sign next to the luxury car read "Anywhere in Vancouver for $35." I handed the hostel flyer to the driver. "Can you take all of us to this address please mate?" I asked him.

He was super friendly. "Wherever you want to go man." He replied, opening the rear door for us all to get inside. About fifteen minutes later we pulled up outside the hostel. We'd been chatting to the driver the whole time and he'd told us where the best places were to have a beer and a good time. Parking at the kerbside he was not impressed with our chosen residence.

"Don't stay here guys!" he advised us. "Let me take you to a nice part of town. You don't want to be hanging around here."

We were too excited to muck about looking for somewhere else. We wanted to get to a pub.

"Here's alright." I said. "it's only seven dollars a night."

He seemed genuinely worried. "Seriously, don't stay here, this place is nasty!" he persisted.

The blokes were already out of the car. We paid him and he left us to it. He was right though, it was a real shit hole and within ten minutes of being there we all agreed that we shouldn't move around on our own, at least staying in pairs for security. There were homeless people everywhere, discarded needles in doorways, and people walking around like zombies, talking to themselves angrily, either drunk or on drugs. Opposite our hostel was a XXX adult cinema, and next door to that a strip club. It was perfect.

That first night we all got extremely drunk and nearly everyone broke the "stay together" rule, returning to the hostel one at a time after wandering around lost for a while. Two of the blokes did come back together, and they ended up walking along the railway tracks for hours, they'd remembered that our hostel was near a railway bridge and in their alcohol impaired wisdom, decided that was the best way to get back. It obviously worked, eventually.

On the third day of that trip we were all suffering with hangovers and decided to lay off the booze until the evening. That didn't last long. We'd been walking around some shops for a short while when someone spotted a sign outside a strip club that got their attention. The billboard showed a stunning woman dressed in sexy lingerie and claimed that she was a Playboy model who worked inside as a pole dancer. In we went, and sure enough there was a woman in lingerie, pole-dancing behind the bar, but it must have been the models day off, because she looked nothing like the picture outside, in fact she looked more like one of the crack addicts that walked the streets by the hostel. We had a couple of overpriced beers and left, huddling outside to decide what to do next. Most of the blokes wanted to carrying on drinking by then, a couple of drinks had whet their appetites and they wanted to go back to Gastown where all the bars were. One bloke wanted to go to a brothel, somehow aroused by the horrendous erotic dancing we'd endured. I'd spotted a harness for weight training earlier in the day and wanted to go back to the sports shop to buy it, and one of the others also wanted to revisit one of the stores so we all agreed a rendezvous and split up. As I walked away one of the blokes in the other group jumped out in the road to stop a taxi driver, who skidded to a halt as he slammed on his brakes. Everyone in the busy street turned to look, as the blokes quickly opened all three doors and hurriedly jumped in. Clearly and loudly, one of them yelled instructions to the driver.

"Take us to the whores!"

The doors slammed shut, and the cab sped away like a getaway car. That scene is embedded deep in my brain. It happened in the space of just a few seconds, like it was rehearsed.

There were some really classy women in Vancouver, but none of them wanted anything to do with us drunken idiots, so instead we got talking to some others, and one of them came back to the hostel with us. She'd probably been evicted from her crack-den or was on day-release from a mental asylum, but even she was concerned about the location of our accommodation as we navigated through the dark streets.

"Where the hell are you taking us man?" she asked nervously as we walked past a man with a tube hanging out of his nose, stumbling down the road towards us. We got back okay, and she spent the night. In the morning I sent her into the room Scotty was sleeping in.

"Go in there and tell Scotty he's a little crow!" I told her, and I listened from outside as she went in.

"Scotty you crew!" she said aggressively.

Scotty wasn't impressed. "What did you call me?" he snapped.

"You fucking crew!" she repeated with authority.

He quickly worked out what had happened and guessed I'd be outside giggling like a four year old. "Steve, get this mong out of my room before I throw her out the fucking window you prick!" he shouted to me before speaking to her again. "Who are you calling a crew anyway? Piss off!"

That night we bumped into that girl again in a different night-club and we got talking. I was really drunk again when she made a confession.

"Remember last night, how I told you I was from Seattle?" she said.

I had no recollection of that whatsoever. "Yes, of course." I replied.

"Well," she continued. "I lied to you. I'm not from Seattle, and I want to be honest. I'm actually from Hollywood."

I was immediately worried. It was obviously a codeword, and my inebriated hypochondriac brain went into overdrive. "What the fuck are you telling me?" I said sharply. "What does that mean?"

"It means I live in Hollywood, not Seattle." she explained.

I was getting anxious now. "Is that a codeword for something?"

She was probably getting anxious now too because of the way I was acting.

I ushered the bartender over. "Hey mate!" I shouted over the noise of the music. "If a girl from round here tells you she's from Hollywood, what does it mean?" I demanded.

He looked at me puzzled. "Well, I guess it means they come from Hollywood." He answered logically.

"Bullshit!" I snapped. "It means they've got fucking AIDS!!" In that moment, with that much alcohol in my body, and my mental state probably a little compromised, that was a logical conclusion. Hollywood starts with H, and AIDS starts with HIV. Her logical conclusion was to get the hell away from the mad Englishman immediately, which she did, and I never saw her again. I never did work out what the codeword meant though.

RESOLUTE BAY

After a few winters in Norway with 3 PARA conducting Arctic warfare training, a cold weather survival course in Sweden with their special forces and operating in the extreme cold on operations in Afghanistan, I thought I was fairly well conditioned to the cold-weather environment. That was until I went to the Canadian High Arctic, where the temperature easily surpassed my previous low of -40°C and reached -55°C. It's so cold there that trees don't even grow, and the North Pole is actually closer than the nearest tree. Attending the extreme cold weather (ECW) survival course run by the Canadian SERE school, we were flown by a military C130 Hercules airplane into Resolute Bay, on Cornwallis Island, which is the location of one of the world's most northern communities. As well as a small Inuit town, Resolute Bay is also home to a large arctic research facility that the Canadian military utilise as a base for running courses. Because of the extreme cold, venturing outside is only permitted when absolutely necessary, and because of the real-time threat of wild Polar Bears, entrances and exits to buildings are always left unlocked, and are all outward opening, so that people can get inside quickly if they are being chased by an angry, ravenous bear. Some days it was so cold there that my eyelids were sticking together when I blinked, and any exposed skin felt like it was actually freezing when the wind touched it. Cigarette lighters, even when kept next to the heat of the body would freeze and become useless within seconds of exposure and batteries died within minutes.

For the course I was teamed up with two SERE instructors from

France, who were also there to develop their own ECW knowledge. Sylvain and Thomas were good blokes and spoke in English whenever I was there, to be polite, even though almost the entire course were French Canadians who all spoke French. In the accommodation block, we were put into rooms by teams, so there were three of us in our room, which had two bunk beds and four small metal lockers. The first night in that room the Frenchmen were abruptly awoken in the middle of the night by a loud, aggressive shout which made them sit bolt upright in their beds. I also woke up, but I was already sitting, on the top bunk, pointing at Sylvain, who was looking at me very worriedly from the bottom bunk of the opposite bed.

"Steve are you okay?" he asked.

I'd been dreaming again and had just screamed out "I can fucking see you!" while pointing right at him.

"Sorry gents, I was having a bad dream." I said and went back to sleep. They were good about it when I apologised to them again in the morning and joked about how I'd scared them awake. All soldiers will know somebody who shouts, fights, or goes for walks in their sleep, and I'm one of them that throws punches, headbutts the pillow and swears a lot. It's not the most relaxing sleep for my wife sometimes.

I woke Thomas up another time after that. This time we were sleeping inside a snow-cave we'd built into the side of a big embankment. Sylvain found it claustrophobic and refused to stay inside, convinced the cave would collapse, and we'd be buried alive. Thomas and I were more confident in our work and settled down for some sleep at the end of a hard day's graft. This time I woke us both up by yelling "Everybody get the fuck out!" A candle was burning in the cave, the flickering flame lighting up the small white space well, so I could see the look of terror on Thomas's face as his head appeared urgently from inside his sleeping bag. If there's a sentence you don't want to hear when you're asleep, naked, inside a sleeping bag, that's inside a bivi bag, in a cave, at the end of a tunnel, with tons of snow above your head, it's probably "Everybody get the fuck out!"

"Sorry mate. Dreaming again." I reassured him. He looked really pissed off this time, I think that really scared him, and afterwards I don't know if he was able to, but I went straight back to sleep.

One day during that course, the instructors gave my team a chance to go for a skidoo ride, and after a quick brief on the machine's controls, off we went. A herd of Musk Ox, had been seen in the area and our guides were keen to show them to us, eventually catching a glimpse of the elusive beasts, that are native to the Tundra of the High Arctic. We also saw remnants of old whaling sites and several inukshuks, which are piles of stones built by the native inuit people to waymark routes, set boundaries, or mark sacred places. The best part for me though, was riding out onto the sea ice. I didn't even realise we were on the frozen Arctic Ocean until I looked back and saw what looked like a coastline.

"Are we on the sea?" I asked, risking looking a bit stupid.

"We sure are." I was informed.

In my defence it wasn't that obvious. It wasn't flat, like I'd expected, but it was flatter than the rest of the ground we'd covered, undulating and uneven where the ice had cracked and pushed upwards under the huge force of the expanding mass. We stopped to have a walk around and I took some photographs, pretty sure I'd never get to do it again. One of the French men knelt next to some blue ice for a photo, then took out a small plastic vial from his pocket and scraped a piece of the ice into it. He had obviously planned to do it and seemed pleased with his prize.

"What are you going to do with that?" I asked him.

"I will take it home to show my children." he replied proudly.

I just nodded, surely he realised it wouldn't be ice anymore when he got back to France! I'm no scientist, but I reckon it would have just been a tiny bit of water.

Throughout that time in Resolute there was always a member of the instructor team armed. When we gathered together as a course for a lesson, at least one man would carry a rifle, and during the night an instructor would be on guard duty, overwatching the small valley we were operating in. In the centre of our training site, for the duration of the exercise, a hand-operated fire alarm was set up on a tripod. We never received a brief on its purpose, and I only found out after the course was finished that it was a bear alarm. Apparently, on identifying a bear, we were supposed to ring it to alert everyone else of the danger. What we were also not told was there was a loaded hunting rifle on the tripod too, and that was for anyone to use against intruder bears. That would never happen in the British military, a loaded weapon left lying around, without people even receiving a familiarisation lesson on it. The last thing you want to be doing is fumbling for a safety catch, when half a ton of Polar Bear is hurtling towards you at twenty-five miles per hour. We never did see a bear, and I was happy with that.

I have seen wild bears once though, during another trip to Canada, this time on the mainland in Goose Bay, Newfoundland. We were on a forward-air-controller exercise, and the sergeant in charge of our small group said there was a place he knew of nearby that was frequented by black bears. Four of us jumped in a 4x4 vehicle and he drove us out to a landfill site where we debussed and jumped over the gate. I'd thought we were going to watch the bears from the safety of the vehicle, but he was relaxed enough and there were several other people in the site too. The other people weren't there to look for bears, they were there collecting plastic bottles from amongst the rubbish and filling huge sacks with them. At the end of the day they'd take them to a collection centre and exchange them for cash. They must have been hard-up. They were probably hoping to get eaten by some bears to put them out of their misery. At the edge of the dump was a pine forest, and as we walked towards it a bear appeared, walking slowly on all fours and seemingly oblivious to our presence. We stood still and watched from a distance of about fifty metres, with masses of rubbish and a ditch separating us, but nothing that would stop an attacking bear. It was amazing to be so close to a wild animal like that, but as much as I was impressed, I was also racking my brains to remember which bear was the infamous Grisly; was it the black, or was it the brown bear? It was a 50/50 question, and I couldn't remember the answer, I just hoped it was the brown. A few seconds after the first bear came two more, but these were smaller, cubs. I'm no zoologist, but I've watched enough David Attenborough to know that animals can be very protective of their young, and this was becoming a worse idea by the second. I looked back towards the truck, it was a few hundred metres away, but on a clear dirt-track, and I reckoned I could get back pretty quick. I looked at the others and felt confident that the bear would get one of them first. I was never going to outrun a bear, but I was confident I'd outrun them. Survival of the fittest!

JORDANIAN FREEFALL FREE-FOR-ALL

Freefall parachuting is taken very seriously in the British military. Training is delivered by RAF Parachute Jump Instructors and conducted in a tightly controlled environment, with multiple layers of safety and competency checks at all levels. After jumping with some soldiers from the Jordanian special forces in 2001, it seemed they were not quite so diligent in their quality assurance. Jumping from a Super-Puma helicopter at 9000 feet, our first combined drop with their soldiers was also our last, because they were absolute maniacs under canopy! Anyone who conducts freefall parachute training in the UK, be it civilian or military, learns from the very beginning that you follow a landing pattern onto the drop zone. Everyone approaches the landing area from the same direction; safe and into wind. This prevents people colliding into each other, which is very dangerous. On the ground there are always wind direction markers, such as flags and windsocks to indicate the direction of the prevailing wind.

That first jump in Jordan was complete chaos, with the Jordanian soldiers flying in to the landing area from all directions. At least half of them took a downwind or a crosswind landing, skidding along the ground on their asses or tumbling head over heels on the sandy floor. Our blokes had to take evasive action to avoid collision and those of us who had time to witness this landed in a completely different place for our own safety. After that we made sure there was a good gap between us and them jumping so we wouldn't have to occupy the same airspace.

After one jump, I noticed the Jordanian parachute instructor reviewing some footage on the small video camera attached to the top of his helmet. He was an experienced skydiver with thousands of jumps and wore a wingsuit, so no doubt he was pretty good. Me and one of my mates walked across inquisitively and peered over his shoulder to have a look. The video was of the last jump he'd done and showed one of the other Jordanians in freefall. Me and my friend looked at each other in horror, the bloke was in absolute tatters! He was spinning around, and tumbling head over heels, with flailing arms and legs. The cameraman stayed right next to him the whole way down, recording the helpless soldier all the way down to pull height, not intervening at all. Even the canopy deployment was shocking to watch, because the man was still tumbling when it came out, and it shot between his legs mid somersault, narrowly avoiding entangling him.

In the British military, someone so unskilled would never be allowed to jump on their own. Our first few freefall jumps are done with instructors holding onto us, only letting go if they are happy with your position, and quickly re-taking their grip if you begin to go unstable. My mate spoke to the cameraman.

"How come you didn't grab hold of him?" he asked.

"No, I do not do that." he replied. "He must change his position. He must learn."

We explained how the RAF PJI's hold onto the students until they are competent, but his answer surprised us.

"He is not a student. He is fully trained." he told us.

The RAF might be a bit anal about parachuting, but at least it's relatively safe.

CHAPTER EIGHT

It Seemed Like A Good Idea At The Time

PRIOR PREPARATION PREVENTS PISS POOR PERFORMANCE

"What the fuck are you doing you absolute maniac!?" Were the words that woke me up one morning in Aldershot. I opened my eyes to a foggy, tunnel-vision view of my good friend Steve Boulton, who was standing over me, leaning forward, and looking at me closely shaking his head. My breathing was a little bit laboured, like a bad impression of Darth Vader, and there was a pressure on my face like someone had been using a sink plunger on it. I'd been sleeping in my respirator / gas mask. I took it off and sat up in my bed, a few droplets of sweat dripping from the inside of it. Steve was laughing.

"Why are you sleeping in your respirator mate? Who the fuck does that!?" he asked.

It was a fair question, nobody likes wearing them, even if it's just for a few minutes, they are really uncomfortable, quite claustrophobic, and very hot.

"I need to get used to wearing it." I replied. We'd been on exercise and had a simulated chemical attack on our position, and for the first time in my life I'd felt the panic of claustrophobia. Running around wearing that mask had got me short of breath and left me feeling extremely vulnerable. I didn't want to be in that position ever again, where my effectiveness as a platoon member was compromised, so I'd decided to condition myself to wearing it. Everyone heard about that, and I got a fair amount of stick for being a freak, but I didn't mind, there were worse things to be known for than being keen.

Before joining the army I thought I should prepare myself for sleeping on the ground as I anticipated doing that a lot. I'd already got rid of my bed to make space for my weights and punchbag, and was using just a mattress, that I'd prop up on its side against the wall every morning. I progressed from that to a blanket, and I'd unfold that every night to sleep on in an attempt to toughen myself up for military service. I also thought it would be a good idea to start running with weight on my back, and my mum bought me a 25kg bag of sand from the builders merchants so I could put it in my old school rucksack, and I began running with that. I had to stop when the straps snapped off under the strain though. Just as well, I doubt it was doing my knees any good.

Something else I did that I knew would be useful, was learn my eight digit, army service number off by heart. It was 25025407 and the way I remembered it was by breaking it down into three parts, 250, 254, 07. To be honest, none of my preparation was of any benefit, and I'd have been much better off learning how to iron instead because that would have saved me hours and hours of work.

 Army recruits don't constantly sleep on the floor in the woods, that only happens when they're on exercise. As it turned out, they have beds, like normal people, and for some reason I always have a great night's sleep in army issue beds. Trying to run with twenty-five kilograms of sand on my back had also been a bit reckless because in Depot our standard weight was thirty pounds, almost half that weight. I'd even managed to memorise my army number wrong, getting quickly, and sternly corrected by my corporal the first time I recited it.
"O is a letter, not a number! Zero is a number! Zero! Not O!" I was informed. Not only that, but army numbers are also given in two

groups of four, not two groups of three and a pair. My number was not 250, 254, 07, it was 2502, 5407. Re-learning that was more difficult than it sounds, just like when someone reads back your phone number in a different rhythm than you are accustomed to, it just sounds wrong.

NO PAIN, NO GAIN

Body modifications are not a new phenomenon. My mates in 3 PARA were pioneering them in the mid 90's, with tattoos, piercings and even some improvised non-surgical enhancement techniques. The first time I ever saw a Prince Albert, where the tip of the penis is pierced with a ring was an old friend called Stan. He had the piercing one weekend and was still in a lot of pain several days later, saying that the swelling was getting worse. In the privacy of the accommodation block Stan showed a few of us his new accessory and we were shocked to see it, reeling backwards with a mixture of responses along the lines of, "Jesus Christ!" "What the fuck!" and "Oh my fucking God!" The end of his penis was swollen to the size of a fist and looked infected.

"Mate you need to take that fucker out!" I said. "That is not good!"

One of the other blokes concurred. "That needs treating Stan! You could lose it!"

Stan seemed a lot less worried than we were, and said he was going to leave it for a few more days to heal up.

"How are you going to keep it sterile?" I asked.

Pulling a surgical rubber glove from his pocket Stan answered, "With this." and stretched the rubber open, before manipulating it over his manhood. It looked insane, like some kind of perverted glove puppet with the fingers and thumb flopping around. Stan explained that he had been using condoms, but they were no longer big enough because of the swelling. Fair play to him though, it did heal.

Another 3 PARA bloke designed his own improvised penis enlarger once, and after just one night his manhood almost doubled in length. Sitting on the top bunk while watching T.V on guard duty, he removed a boot and tied it to his penis, using the laces. After a few minutes he added some weight by placing an apple into the boot and continued doing this until it was full. To the amusement of the others he somehow managed to fall asleep sat there, and they deliberately kept the noise down by whispering and tip-toeing around to avoid waking him up. After a while he did awaken to find he had definitely increased his length, but at the sacrifice of girth, his dick looked like a salami stick, very long, but extremely thin. Apparently it stayed like that for a few hours, before returning to normal.

Falling asleep while wearing a passive training device is even more likely when alcohol is involved, as one of the other blokes discovered. In his quest for a six-pack, he'd invested in an ab-trainer, which was a belt that wrapped around the waist and delivered small electric pulses to the abdomen, causing tight contractions of the muscles. Returning from a night out he decided to do a quick session before he got his head down. He woke up the next morning with stomach cramps to find that he'd fallen asleep with it on, and it was still going. He'd done the equivalent of eight thousand sit-ups and was in agony for days afterwards.

In Long Kesh Camp, Northern Ireland, we were sat around one night when a friend of mine discovered a Slendertone in the locker of another soldier who was at home on Leave. This electric muscle-toning device had several round, sticky pads that you could place anywhere on your body to target specific muscles. Mac, an extremely fit Scotsman took the lead, and we all had a laugh watching his arms contract so tightly he was shouting in pain. It didn't take long to escalate as we took turns, trying the pads on different parts of the body and watching the involuntary contractions bend or straighten our limbs. We even gave the controller to one of the others and let them decide the intensity level, which obviously went straight to level ten. Mac put them on his ass cheeks and tried walking around as they went into spasm, then he put them on each side of his head. His reaction from that was the best, he shouted, his face contorted, and he ripped them off frantically. We were in hysterics.

"Have a go at that Steve." He said, offering the pads to me.

"No thanks, you're alright." I replied.

Him and the others egged me on, and although I hate electricity, I gave in.

"Alright, I'll do it. But only if I can hold the controller!" I stated. I only wanted a small shock.

"Fuck off!"

"Bollox!"

"No way Brown. You know the rules!" Came the immediate replies from the newly, self-appointed adjudicators.

Mac held the controller. "I'll screw the nut mate." He said sincerely. "I'll put it on level three." He showed me the dial as he turned it to level three.

As the others watched, I nervously stuck the pads to my temples with my already sweaty hands.

Mac started counting down. "Three.. Two" He cranked that dial up to ten before he finished counting and sent a horrendous shock into my skull that felt like a bolt of lightning. I don't know why I let him have that controller, it was obvious he was going to do that, and everyone was cracking up watching me squirm. I grabbed the sticky pads and yanked them off, but then got another shock, this time into my fingertips as I tried to shake them off. That was really funny, but a horrible feeling. However Mac upped it one more level when he put them on his nut-sack. Nobody else went that far, his reaction was exactly how you would imagine it to be. It looked torturous, but ultimately he won that game.

PIERCINGS, TATTOOS, AND BUNGEE JUMPS

After a jungle training package in Belize, one of the sergeants from my company called Moggy organised a trip to Cancun, Mexico. The adventure training packages organised by the headquarters were good, and included scuba diving expeditions, sea kayaking and relaxing on Caribbean islands but Cancun sounded better to me and fifteen others, who filled a minibus and drove from Belize City to the Mexican border. Crossing that border was an experience in itself. It was represented by a barrier across the road, a single storey windowless building and a group of dishevelled soldiers in olive green combats and peaked caps. The guards looked more like a militia from an episode of the A-Team than a border force, and they walked around menacingly with their weapons slung behind their backs or carried by their side lazily in one hand. Halted at the barrier, we were ordered off the vehicle and directed towards the building where a small queue of other travellers was waiting for a passport check. Moggy had done this before and told us to take our kit with us and not leave anything on the minibus. We all travelled light and carried our daysacks into the building to join the back of the queue. Within seconds the guards swarmed into the transport and hurriedly searched it for contraband / anything worth stealing, looking under the seats, in the glove-box, and the seat pockets. Inside the building the procedure was simple enough; You presented your passport for inspection to the heavily sweating officer who stood beneath a pathetically slow-turning fan on the ceiling. He stared at you intensely for a second before suspiciously looking you up and down, then handed you back your passport. Next, there was a button on the desk that you had to push, which "randomly" illuminated either a green or red light. A green light meant that you could carry on unimpeded, and a red light meant that you were given a physical search. Ahead of us in the line were about ten Mexicans who showed their passports, and against all odds, each received a green light, moving quickly through and returning to their vehicle outside. Our first bloke went through and sure enough, he got a red light, making us all laugh as he was taken to one side to be frisked down, and his pockets and daysack emptied. The second bloke pressed the button, same detail, third bloke goes through, red light again. It didn't take us long to realise that every time one of us pressed the button, the guards hand reached under the desk on his side to press his own button. All sixteen of us got the red light and were searched, with a fair few U.S dollars disappearing in the process, but no harm done and eventually getting on our way. After a long drive through the whole day we arrived in Cancun and to our delight, found out it was American Spring Break, and absolutely heaving with drunk students.

To save money we shared hotel rooms and had three blokes for each double room, working on a first-come-first-served basis for who got the bed and who got the floor. The first night, we got absolutely hammered, drinking copious amounts of lager and tequila shots. Partying in our short shorts and t-shirts from our P.T kit, the Americans were a bit disturbed by our fashion sense, but we were equally unimpressed with theirs too. Massively oversized shorts that hung below the knee, with socks pulled up high, baseball caps, baggy t-shirts and sandals made grown men look like children. In a nightclub we went into, there was a monkey outside who you could get a photo with, which we couldn't resist, and he was trained to give the middle finger and smile for each shot. Inside there were several levels and bars which were all crowded with people having a good time but every time you bought a drink at the bar, the staff would try and rip you off, either short-changing you, or walking off completely. Tequila shots were also readily available to buy, from people walking around carrying trays full of them. One of the servers was a dwarf in a poncho and sombrero, but the most popular was a woman in hot pants and a tiny t-shirt. She'd wedge the shot glass in her cleavage, and you'd have to get it without using your hands.

I woke up in the morning to the voice of my friend Bosh. Three of us were on the bed, me in the middle, Bosh on my right, and Scotty on my left.

"What the fuck!?" Bosh exclaimed, quickly followed by another. "What the fuck!?" There was a slight pause, then a louder, high pitched yelp. "What the fuck!?"

I opened my eyes to see Bosh sat on the edge of the bed with his back to me, feet on the floor, looking downwards. He'd woken up to see blood on his top, then realised he'd had his nipple pierced, hence the shock.

"What's the matter mate?" I asked.

Bosh stood up and turned around slowly to face me, he was wide eyed and white as a sheet. Pointing to his groin he pulled his bloodied shorts to the side and chuckled, "What the fuck is that all about?"

Not only was his nipple pierced, with a silver ring through it, his bell-end was also pierced with a Prince Albert, and that also was covered in congealed blood.

I burst out laughing straight away. "You fucking idiot!" I said. "Where did you get that done?"

We were both laughing. "I have no idea, I can't remember anything!" he answered.

The noise had woken Scotty who immediately noticed an addition to his body too.

"Ahhh, what the fuck is that!?" he groaned. "For fucks sake!"

Scotty was the funniest bloke I ever met, and he had me in

stitches all the time with his antics. I turned to see what stupidity he might have pulled off and he was now sat on his side of the bed with his back to me. I was still laughing about Bosh, but now me and Bosh were looking at him in anticipation. Scotty stood up and turned to face us, grinning broadly.

"I think that's a real tattoo!" he said, pointing to his belly button and rubbing at the writing around it.

I was belly laughing now, literally crying. "You're not from Grimsby!" I spluttered.

"No, but my dad is." he replied, like it was a justification for the "Made in Grimsby" tattoo above and below his belly button. He also had no recollection of getting the work done.

That night I got my nipple pierced too and I think the only reason I remember it, is because it was so painful! I remember sitting down in an open air studio, taking my t-shirt off, and saying, "pierce that fucker!" as I pointed to my nipple. Probably due to my inebriated state and arrogance I was given zero pain relief, not even a cheeky rub from an ice cube to numb it before the man pushed a needle straight through my nipple horizontally. Two Americans watched on curiously and one of them asked me, "Hey man, doesn't that hurt?" He was obviously surprised by my lack of reaction.

"No mate, it's buckshee." I slurred. It was then the man started to push the ring through the hole he'd just made, and that was outrageously painful, despite the gallons of lager and tequila. "Aaaaarrrggghhhh! Jeeeesus Chhhrrist!" I growled through gritted teeth. I looked back at the Americans, "Cancel that! It really hurts!" I said. Apparently, earlier that night I'd been trying to convince my mate Sean to come and get a piercing through our penises, telling him that we should do it together, because we were brothers, and it was airborne, blah blah blah. Thankfully, he was a fraction more sensible than me and declined, so I obviously bottled it and got the nipple done instead, taking it out when I sobered up the following day because it looked ridiculous. We got so drunk on that trip we were even doing bungee jumps and forgetting about them until receiving a video of it, delivered to the hotel from the bungee company. Good times.

THE LAST LEG

On Friday 13th April 2001 a good friend of mine smashed his femur, the biggest bone in the human body, in a nasty parachuting accident. Stu had started skydiving after me but doing it on civilian drop zones and using civilian equipment he was advancing quickly, not having the strict control measures and constraints that the military have. It wasn't long before he bought his own parachute, and when he told me about it I was surprised that he was already capable of handling such a small canopy, with the dynamic performance specifications it had. Military canopies are normally quite big and more designed to get you down safely, rather than dangerously fast and flashy, and I knew I wasn't competent enough to jump with that size parachute yet despite having more experience than him.

"Be careful with that mate." I said. "That's going to be a bit cheeky!"

The blokes who saw his accident at the drop zone in Israel, said he came in at such a dynamic turn, his parachute hit the ground before his body did. Stu had a massive metal rod inserted into his left thigh to keep it all together and eventually got back to full fitness. When the rod was removed he had it framed and hung it on the wall in his room. On the 6th of September 2006 Stu had more grief with that leg, but this time the bone couldn't be screwed back together, because it was obliterated into a thousand pieces, and scattered across the Afghan desert. Part of the ill-fated Kajaki patrol, that was later made into a movie, Stu was terribly wounded by a landmine that resulted in the amputation of his left leg, from above the knee. Despite massive wounds to his right leg, doctors managed to save that, leaving it badly scarred but functional. At one point, while Stu was in hospital, his dad was told there was a 90% chance the right leg would be amputated too. The Afghan conflict saw many soldiers like Stu return home with life changing injuries, both physical and psychological, and their unfortunate sacrifices drove research and development in medical treatments and technologies to totally new levels. Stu himself was at the forefront of this advancement, undergoing intense physical rehabilitation and receiving a prosthetic leg.

Stu continued parachuting after his injuries had healed and travelled to the U.S.A to jump at Elsinore drop zone in California a couple of times. On 1st of April 2013 a few days after jumping with the Red Devils parachute display team, he broke his other leg. Normally, he'd deliberately land on his ass to avoid damaging the prosthetic and remaining leg, but a gust of wind blew him sideways at the last second, and he instinctively reached out with his foot, snapping the shin bone in half. When the emergency services arrived to treat him, Stu was surprised at the impressive turnout. Americans don't do things by halves, and accompanying the ambulance was the local Sheriff and Fire Service. He was especially surprised to see the firefighters and his dry sense of humour kicked in.
"Don't tell me I'm on fucking fire too!?" he shouted. Apparently they didn't think he was funny. To be fair, I doubt they understood a word he said.

TALE OF THE TAPE

Issued black duct tape is literally what holds the British armed forces together, well the equipment anyway. Nicknamed "Black Nasty" or "Bodge Tape" amongst the army in recognition of the less aesthetic jobs it's been used for, it can be relied on by soldiers, sailors, and airmen to perform a plethora of tasks. Whether it's for securing a naked young soldier to a lamp post outside in the rain or repairing a damaged rotor blade on a Chinook helicopter, a roll of Black Nasty is an essential item on the packing list for any military operation. I wouldn't even be surprised if the Royal Navy use it to plug holes in their nuclear submarines. In fact they do! FACT! [1] Any self-respecting serviceperson that knows somebody in the store, or who has access to it, has a roll of this in their bedspace / house, right next to the stash of AA batteries they've nicked. [2]

Useful applications for Black Nasty:
Improvised "Hitler tache" for fancy dress. (3 PARA Anti-tank Platoon)
Improvised plaster / band aid
Improvised wrapping paper tape
Improvised candle
Improvised handcuffs
Clothing repair
Tent repair
Land Rover canopy repair
Boot repair
Football puncture repair

Holding the soldiers together is the distant cousin of Black Nasty, another kind of tape that has been used for decades to prevent, treat, cure, and conceal injuries; Zinc-Oxide Tape. It is said, that if you laid ou, all the zinc oxide tape that's applied to the feet and backs of Depot Para recruits every year, it would be enough to fill a thousand Olympic swimming pools, be as long as a million double-decker buses, or cover an area the size of Wales. *3

When you join the army and start running around in brand new boots, with a bergan (rucksack) on, there is a good chance you'll suffer "bergan burns" and blisters. The friction from a bergan rubbing against your back for hours on end can cause painful sores and friction burns, that if left untreated, can become infected. New, leather boots can also cause debilitating injuries to a recruit, and blisters on the soles, heels, instep, toes, or arches are very common. I'd read about this before I joined up and tried to prepare myself by wearing Doc Martin boots everywhere. They were the most highly polished boots you've ever seen on a civilian, as I tried to get myself ready for Depot. To break those boots in, I tried all the different methods that were recommended in the books I had. I soaked them in the bath, walked though streams, and even urinated into them, as recommended by the "experts" in my literature. I also learned how to treat blisters from those books, and threaded a length of cotton through several, leaving it hanging out to slowly drain the fluid. Little did I know, all I needed was a good supply of zinc oxide tape. In Depot there were blokes half-covered in the stuff. Some people had great big patches of it on their backs, and they'd leave it on there for a week at a time. Usually it would be hastily stuck directly to the wound, so removing it would be very painful, and re-open the sores. Some peoples feet were almost entirely wrapped in the stuff like a sock. I think everyone used it at one point or another. Taking the tape off was often best done by someone else, someone you trusted to do it quickly. Doing it yourself could be torturous because you'd naturally want to do it slowly to avoid the pain. Yanking it off in one rapid movement was by far the better option, and it was entertaining for others to watch too.

One part of the body that you should never, ever, under any circumstances have zinc oxide tape applied to though, and I say this from personal experience, is the tip / glans of the penis. In Sierra Leone, after a long patrol though the jungle, that part of my body became really sensitive and sore, and I put it down to the brand new cycling shorts I was wearing because weren't 100% lycra like my old ones. I spent the next day getting as much air to it as possible, dropping my pants randomly when there were no locals about, and putting plenty of army issue foot powder on it. After a while I could stand it no longer, every time it touched any material it was like someone stubbing out a cigarette on my bell end. That was when I reverted to my medical, self-help, default setting and deployed the zinc oxide. I carefully taped over my glans, using small strips of the adhesive white material, so that it could "swell" without cutting off the blood supply if it decided to. There wasn't much to get excited about in the jungle, but I was having a lot of vivid dreams while taking the Larium anti-malarial tablets. As always, the tape worked, and I kept it on for the next few days until we were withdrawn from the village and moved back to Freetown to fly home. The airport was very busy, with hundreds of British troops waiting for their flights. Every seat was taken, and every bit of space had people or equipment lying on it. There was nowhere private to do it, so I decided to remove my dressing right there, in the terminal. I did my best to keep it discrete and a couple of mates tried to shield me, but a few of the 1 PARA blokes watched on in disbelief, laughing and grimacing at the same time as I pulled the strips off one by one. This was one job that had to be done by me, and slowly. I was sweating from the pain. One of the blokes who saw my ordeal came over and asked me why the hell I'd used the tape in the first place, and I told him what happened. He suggested it was probably thrush and got me some cream which I applied immediately. It worked, and it was much easier to apply than the tape. I wonder if I'm the only person in the world stupid enough to have done that?

*1 - Not a fact
*2 - Allegedly
*3 - Not independently verified

PARAS AND MARINES

When I was a kid I asked my mum what the difference was between the Paras and the Marines. I'd watched documentaries on both, where they followed recruits through training, and both had claimed to be the best. My mum explained it from her perspective. "The Paras are really good, but they are totally crazy. When they go into battle they just jump straight in without even thinking about it." She said.

The Marines are really good too, but they are more sensible and nicer. They take their time and make sure things are done properly."

That early advice helped shape my future, the Paras sounded much more exciting!

When I went to Norway with 3 PARA for the first time, a lot of the initial arctic warfare instruction was delivered by Mountain Leaders, ML's, from the Royal Marines who are the UK's foremost experts in that field. During an early lesson on our Arctic Ski and Survival Course we were told about the use of ski wax and how to apply it to the skis. The ML melted some wax and showed us how to apply it to the underside of the issue "planks." At the end of the lesson he explained that we needed to do the same process to our own skis that night, in preparation for our first practical lesson the following morning. He'd used a small electric machine to melt his wax but none of us had one. A hand went up in the audience. "How are we supposed to melt the wax?" one of the Paras asked.

The ML answered confidently, using his personal experience. "It's really easy guys, you use your iron." he explained. "Plug it in, turn it upside down, put a mess tin, or maybe a cleaned out bean tin on top, and melt it in that."

Another hand went up. "What if we haven't got an iron?" came the question.

The ML seemed slightly surprised at that query. "Well, just use your mates iron instead." He said.

We were looking around at each other, all thinking the same thing when a third question was asked. "What if nobody has got an iron, is there somewhere else we can all melt the wax?"

The ML was still getting used to working with us lot. "Lads, there are fifty of you in here, I'm sure between all of you, somebody here has got an iron!"

Our blank looks and deathly silence showed our lack of confidence in that notion. He addressed the room to help out. "Hands up if you have an iron." He called out.

Not a single hand was raised, as we sat there wondering how we were going to melt that wax when it was minus fifteen degrees outside, and we weren't even allowed to light fires.

"Come on lads" he pleaded, "You must have irons with you for Christ's sake."

One of our blokes replied from the back of the classroom. "Why would anyone bring an iron with them to Norway?"

The ML was genuinely puzzled. "How do you iron your uniform then?"

"We don't! There's no straight lines in nature!" one of the blokes shouted out to our amusement. Everything we packed when we went away was essential, and everything that was essential was made as light as possible. We had a limited baggage allowance and limited space, luxury items were CD Walkman's, books, and porn magazines, not irons. Unable to comprehend the idea that we didn't iron our uniform while living in the mountains of the Arctic, the ML had one more query.

"What are you going to do if you get a run ashore?" he said, using Navy "Jack-Speak" to ask how we'd iron our civvies for a night out. Most of us knew what he meant, but we weren't going to humour him by acknowledging his foreign language.

"We are ashore!" he was told.

In my final years in the Army I became friends with the most senior Mountain Leader in the Royal Marines, a bloke called Andy. By the time we met we were both in our forties, and both probably a lot more mellow than we were as youngsters, so we got on well. One day we were talking about pet hates, and I mentioned to him about Marines getting upset by people shaving, while wearing a t-shirt. Andy is a really chilled out bloke who speaks with a very deep, but fairly quiet voice.
"Yeah that really winds me up mate!" he said. "I don't get it at all. Why would anyone do that? It's dirty, it's lazy, I hate it!"
Personally that kind of thing doesn't bother me at all, I couldn't care less what people wear in the ablutions. "Well I don't do it either, but maybe people do it because they're cold or something?" I stated. "I just wouldn't want to get shaving cream on my t-shirt."
Andy explained to me how he'd been shaving in the ablutions on an army camp once, and a bloke had stood at the sink next to his, and also started shaving, while still wearing a t-shirt. Realising Andy was a Marine the bloke had joked, "I bet you hate people like me who keep their tops on when they shave, don't you Royal?"
Andy described his thought process to me. "I looked at that bloke," he said, "and he hadn't done anything to me, but I was so fucking wound up by him shaving like that, so angry. And do you know what I realised mate?" he asked me.
I genuinely thought he was going to say that he realised it was trivial, and not worth getting worked up about.
"What's that mate?" I replied.
He continued, in a different direction to what I'd anticipated. "I realised that I wanted to smash his fucking head off that sink and stomp on his stupid fucking face!" he said sincerely.
That cracked me up and I had to tell him I wasn't expecting that. I like it when other soldiers are as brainwashed as me.

STEVE BROWN

An old sweat in 3 PARA told me a story once, about a group of Royal Marines who went for a beer in a strictly "Parachute Regiment Only" bar in Aldershot. They were in town for the night and ventured in to a pub called 5's. Apparently one of the blokes approached them, told them of their error, and advised them to leave promptly. Ignoring his advice the Marines ordered themselves a beer and carried on, drawing the attention of everyone in there. Massively outnumbered it was a poor decision and made worse by the fact they'd been given the option to leave peacefully, an offer not often afforded to trespassers. Predictably a fight ensued, and the Marines took a hiding, although they did put up an impressive fight in the enemies own territory. Later that night the blokes had moved on to the Rat Pit and were enjoying a beer in there when one of the Marines reappeared. Bold as brass he walked up to one of the blokes involved in the earlier fight. "We're not happy with what happened before, we want another go. We'll be outside."

Listening to that story you had to respect those Marines. It was like a group of Paras kicking off in a pub in Plymouth, they were never going to win. I asked my mate what happened next, expecting him to say that the blokes were so impressed by their sheer recklessness and fighting spirit they called a truce, and all got drunk together. Yeah. That didn't happen.

"They got fucking battered again mate, but much worse than the first time." He told me.

THE PROFESSOR

As a Private soldier in 3 PARA in the mid 1990's it was highly unusual to have an academic degree and the post-nominals BSc. We had one such bloke in A Company, who's relative genius compared to the rest of us earned him the nickname "The Professor" or "Prof". As a new bloke Prf didn't initially endear himself to some members of his platoon, and when he shunned their first invitation to join them for a drink down town, some took offense. One such soldier was a lance corporal called Jay, and when he returned fom his night out, he went to visit Prof, who was still awake, sat in bed reading a book. Jay was a super keen, airborne-all-the way, fully indoctrinated paratrooper, who loved his regiment and the airborne brotherhood. He also loved to tell you how much he loved his regiment and the airborne brotherhood, especially after a few pints.

On seeing Prof in bed, and clearly sober, Jay took it upon himself to explain to him the importance of going out with the blokes.
"We've been out drinking, fighting, and scoring with chicks, while you've been here reading this shit! he said, taking the book and tossing it across the room. Jay's personal library was exclusively books about the Paras, the S.A.S, famous airborne battles, and guns.
"We live together, and we die together, because we are brothers. On the battlefield I will die for my brother, and he will die for me." Jay would talk like this for hours when he was drunk, he meant it, but when you were listening to it, and sober, it was a nightmare. Prof was sober, and very intelligent, but when Jay carried on, and told him he'd just drunk ten pints of lager, his

judgement failed him.

"And that makes you hard does it?" Prof said sarcastically.

Jay lost it. Dragging Prof out of his bed he proceeded to give him a beating, which included smashing his head into the reinforced glass window in a door, shattering it and bruising Prof's head. The following morning Prof was summoned to the office of the Company Quartermaster Sergeant, a colour sergeant who's nickname was "The Gasket" because of his tendency to get very angry. The Gasket had heard about the previous night's shenanigans and wanted to get to the bottom of it, to ensure appropriate disciplinary action could be taken against the offender. Sporting a black eye and some swelling to his head, Prof spoke briefly to The Gasket who quickly analysed the situation, and apportioned blame.

"You owe me forty pounds for a new window you chopsy little shit! Think yourself lucky I'm not charging you for vandalism you fucking crow!" he told him. I think that style of management is what's commonly known as "Firm, but fair!?"

In 1994, Prof and I attended a communications course in 3 PARA. There were twelve students on the course, and the lessons were delivered by communications specialists from the Signals Platoon, who were responsible for establishing and maintaining radio comms across the battalion, up to Brigade Headquarters , and with any other units working within the battle group. One of the instructors was a lance corporal called Robbo, an extremely keen and proficient soldier, who had joined the British army from his home country of New Zealand. Robbo was teaching us about how the F1 and F2 layers of the ionosphere merged at night, and how that had an adverse effect on high-frequency (HF) comms. As far as lessons go, that one is pretty dry, especially to a bunch of blokes who thought the ionosphere was a nightclub in Bracknell. Prof however, was in his element, this was like day one, week one of university for him, and while the rest of us nodded along, pretending to understand this science fiction, he was contemplating problems at a much more strategic level. His hand went up, and the room went quiet. I was hoping he was about to ask Robbo to go through it again, this time in laymans terms, because my brain was melting, making me agitated and restless.

"Have you got a question Professor?" Robbo asked.

Prof's hand dropped back down to his desk as he spoke. "Yes please. Could you please explain how the electro-magnetic pulse from an exo-atmospheric explosion would affect spacewave comms?"

It was a genuine question, and probably a very good one, but to most of us, he might as well have been talking Mandarin Chinese. Everyone's stunned gaze shifted from Prof to Robbo to see how he handled that curve-ball.

"Shut up Prof, you fucking smart arse!" Robbo replied. He was good, but not that good.

THE GREAT ATTACK
OF DOVER CASTLE

Dover Castle is a huge fortress, claimed to be the largest castle in England. It was built in 1180 A.D and has survived several sieges and attacks over nine centuries. It has high walls, a deep moat, and a limited number of entry and exit points. However, this great history and impregnable reputation is insignificant to two young paratroopers filled with ten pints of Stella Artois and the accompanying sense of invincibility that comes with it. In my defence it was Mac's idea, not mine.

"Let's break into the castle!" he suggested, as we walked up the steep hill to camp after a good night in town. Connaught Barracks, where we lived, was located next to the castle, on the other side of the road that went from Dover town centre towards Canterbury. It was said to be haunted, and a few of the blokes claimed to have seen ghosts on top of the walls or in the arrow slit windows, although the shadowy ghouls only ever seemed to expose themselves to extremely drunk people. To me there was only one response to such an idiotic proposal.

"Yes! Mega idea!" I said.

Using our elite skills and deep knowledge of structural vulnerabilities, we planned our assault in meticulous detail as we descended into the moat, slipping, and sliding down the steep embankment.

"We'll climb through the window!" Mac declared. It was as simple as that.

The outer wall was illuminated with bright floodlights placed in the moat and as we crossed them our shadows were cast against the stone surface. Reaching the base of the wall was difficult enough, grabbing hold of weeds and tufts of grass to prevent us sliding back down. Mac pointed to a narrow window about twenty feet up a turret.

"I'll climb through that, then go round to the door, and let you in." he explained.

I put my back to the wall and created a stirrup with my hands to give him a bunk-up. "This is gonna be mega!" I chuckled. I'd never been in the castle before and was excited at the idea of exploring the old tunnels and chambers.

Mac put his foot in my hands, and I gave him a boost up the wall as he began the ascent, gripping onto small cracks and protruding stones as he hauled himself up, using my shoulders and head as steps. He got to the window and clung onto the bottom of it, kicking off the wall to scramble up and look inside.

"I think I can fit through." He shouted down to me. He couldn't! The whole point of the narrow windows was to prevent people climbing through them, especially people like him, with massive shoulders you could have landed a helicopter on.

I shouted back up. "Can you see how high from the ground you are?" We were assuming there was a staircase on the inside, but we were guessing.

"It's pitch black. I'll just hang and jump." Mac answered, looking into complete darkness. We never found out. Fortunately, as Mac tried to squeeze his four foot wide shoulders through the one foot wide window he slipped, and came plummeting down, desperately trying to grab hold of something as he fell. In an ambitious attempt to catch him, I outstretched my arms upwards, but crumpled under the fourteen stones of Scotsman, and tumbled head over heels alongside him to the bottom of the moat.

Plan B was immediately formed and launched: Kick the front door in. Amazingly uninjured, we adapted our method of entry and opted for the good old fashioned, tried and tested, brute force technique. Climbing out of the moat we made our way to the main entrance. A huge, medieval, wooden door, with metal fixtures that looked like they'd been hand-crafted by a black-smith hundreds of years before, was all that stood in our way. Mac took one look at it and sat down on a wall.

"There's no way we're getting through that bastard!" he said dejectedly.

Next to that door was a big brown tourist sign, full of facts about the castle. One of those facts was that in all of its history, it had never been conquered. I imagine people have tried all sorts of things on that entrance; battering rams, axes, maybe even canons. Stupidly, I tried kicking it! I hadn't practiced any kickboxing for a few years, but thanks to the ridiculous amount of lager in my bloodstream, I felt pretty confident I still had some skills. Mac watched on unimpressed as I tried a front kick, side kick, and spinning back-kick on the thick, reinforced, oak panelled door. It was a pathetic attempt that achieved nothing except speed up the deterioration of my joints and ligaments as I bounced off the solid structure. I gave up, and joined Mac sat on the wall, where we spent a while waffling on about how impressive the castle was, and what it would have been like to attack it back in the old days, before we walked away defeated to camp.

The next morning I woke up to see my clothes in a heap on the floor, covered in grass stains and mud. Remembering what we'd done I went straight to see Mac, who had his own private bunk in the corridor. Still asleep, his clothes were also on the floor in a discarded heap. I woke him up and passed him his jeans, which had green scuffs from the moat all over them.

"Do you remember what we did last night?" I said as he sat up and took the trousers from me.

He looked puzzled for a moment, then the penny dropped. "What a pair of stupid bastards!" he said, and we both burst out laughing.

ACHTUNG! SCHNELL MEIN DEUTSCHE KAMERADEN!

(Attention! Faster my German comrades)

The Pathfinder's selection course is notoriously difficult, and the majority of those who attempt it will regrettably fail. Most soldiers who volunteer for the course are physically fit and highly motivated individuals, but many are still surprised by the harsh demands placed on them during the six-week package. Before one course, around 2002 we were informed that two soldiers from the German army were attending. This was highly unusual, because there was no prospect of them joining the unit if they were successful, and there was no formal qualification to be gained from completing the course either. It seemed odd that anyone would do the course just for the sake of it, but we were told that was the case, and to treat them the same as every other student attending. No special treatment.

On the first morning of the course we always conducted the army's standard eight-mile speed march. Carrying forty pounds of equipment and a rifle, the march was completed in 2 hours, as per army regulations, over the undulating terrain of Sennybridge Training Area, Wales. This event was only done as part of the safe system of training, a box ticking exercise that ensured all attendees were of a minimum standard of fitness before the real training began, and nobody was expected to fail. In comparison to the other fitness tests on the course, this was by far the easiest. Day two was another eight miler, nicknamed the "PF Express" but this time they'd be carrying fifty-five pounds, and the pace would be much faster, with a cut-off time of 1 hour, 30 minutes. Also in the first week they would complete the army swimming test, with a pool beasting thrown in, a ten-mile speed march carrying forty pounds, in a time of 1 hour 45 minutes, and a two-mile race with full equipment.

On this particular course, the Germans were clearly under-prepared; psychologically and physically. The instructor set off on the first eight-miler at a fast walk, following a tarmac road up a gentle incline which gradually became steeper, then turned at a junction to begin a steady descent. At the top of the hill he called out the warning. "Prepare to double!"
As briefed, the students repeated the call. "Prepare to double!" they shouted in unison, nervously anticipating the increase in pace.
"Double march!" the instructor yelled and began to run.
As the group moved off apace, one soldier started to immediately fall back, and wearing German camouflage it was easy to identify him as one of our guests. One of our safety staff went alongside him to offer some encouragement.
"Come on mate, keep up. Don't let the gap start already!" he said. The German soldier was already looking fatigued, and we were less than a mile into the march.
"Dis is unbelieeeevable!" he said dejectedly, obviously surprised by the speed they were moving.
Loads of us heard that, it was really funny, and great for morale, and that phrase was repeated for years afterwards during hard activities, always delivered in an exaggerated, comical German accent.
With a bit of help from the staff he caught up with the group as they slowed down into a walk for another ascent. Joining in at the back we told him. "Stay with the pack now. Don't fall back."
There is a fair amount of technique to speed-marching, moving

the legs quickly while carrying weight is not easy and takes practise and despite his best efforts, the German soldier could not walk that fast. Every few steps he was continuously switching between walking and running, working extremely hard to keep with the pace. Frustrated, he looked at the safety staff as we walked effortlessly next to him.

"How do you move your legs so quickly?!" he cried despairingly; and another private joke was born.

Shortly after that we withdrew him from the march and put him in the safety vehicle. He was never going to make it round. To his credit, the other German soldier completed the route, he was much fitter than his friend, but had also bitten off more than he could chew.

Back in camp we visited the Germans in their accommodation to check they were okay. They'd been talking to the other blokes on the course and were concerned about their suitability for it. As instructors we were surprised at their naivety.

"Not being funny, but what did you expect?" one of my friends asked. "It's only going to get harder from now on." he warned.

The shell-shocked Germans explained to us how they'd come to be on the course. "We thought we were coming to the U.K for some adventure training!" one of them said. Back home an officer had asked their platoon for volunteers to take part in a course in England, and when asked what the course was about, he'd told them it was some kind of adventure training, with lots of hill walking. There certainly was lots of hill walking, about 300km of it, albeit in the Welsh Mountains of the Brecon Beacons and Black Mountain, but adventure training it was definitely not. Who says the Germans don't have a sense of humour!?

After learning that we put them through a modified version of the course, giving them a reprieve on some of the more intense serials and a bit of time off to enjoy themselves. They loved it. Probably.

(VERY) ACCELERATED FREEFALL COURSE

A friend of mine in 3 PARA called Tommy once told me a story about his first and only ever skydive experience. He was on exercise in Bavaria, when the German paratroopers, the Fallschirmjager hosted a barbecue for the Brits. In my experience, the Germans are brilliant hosts; they love a hog roast, never run out of beer, and always make sure your glass is full. Also in my experience, British soldiers are nightmare guests; they love free food, try their best to drink all the beer, and use empty glasses as projectiles at the first sign of a fight. During the barbecue, the Germans asked if anyone was freefall parachute trained, because they had a jump the following morning and some spare parachutes. Tommy, in his drunken wisdom raised his hand. "I'm freefall trained." he declared. "I'll do it." He was lying, he'd never done a skydive in his life.

Still half-cut in the morning, Tommy paraded at the designated time, and was given a parachute. Never having donned one before, he looked at the others as they put theirs on and tried to imitate what they did. With the reality of the situation dawning on him, and sobering up at a rapid rate, Tommy sidled up to one of the Germans.
"Which handle do I need to pull for the parachute mate?" he asked quietly.
The German looked at him suspiciously. "You don't know how the parachute works?"
he replied, obviously surprised at the query about basic para-

chute operation.

Tommy was committed. "Yeah, we don't have this type in the UK mate. I just want to make sure it works the same as ours do." he bluffed convincingly.

The German soldier accepted his explanation and quickly explained the use of the handles on the parachute harness, pointing deliberately to the ones on Tommy's chest one at a time as he spoke.

"Main canopy. Cut away pad. Reserve canopy." he stated clearly.

"Roger that." Tommy acknowledged. "Exactly the same as ours back home."

Somehow, he managed to get on that plane without anyone detecting his total cluelessness and before long they were airborne, climbing quickly to a jump height of 9,000 feet. When the tailgate was lowered Tommy stood up with the others and moved towards the ramp, catching a glimpse of the view as he walked unsteadily. The jumps he'd done before were from a side-door at eight-hundred feet and he'd only got to look outside for the second before exit. Suddenly he felt sick.

The green light came on and the Germans started leaping out, but Tommy had other ideas and grabbed hold of the seating on the side of the interior. He'd changed his mind; it wasn't for him after all.

The dispatcher beckoned him to the ramp. "Come on. You must jump!" he shouted, waving his arms urgently.

Tommy shook his head, clinging on to the webbing straps of the seat, petrified. "I'm not doing it!" he yelled back.

"Yes! Jump now!" the crewman insisted.

Tommy looked out into the void once more. "Fuck you! I'm not jumping!" he snapped.

"You are an English coward!" screamed the dispatcher, pointing at him angrily.

Even in his state of blind panic, Tommy wasn't having that, and in defiance he stood up straight and sprinted out the back of the plane, with a parting "Fuck you!" to the German, tumbling out of control for a few seconds before locating and pulling his main canopy handle. Fortunately, his parachute paid out nicely, and he was able to work out how to steer it towards the landing zone where he could see the others. Landing nowhere near the X with a parachute landing fall, like taught for normal, static line parachuting, he at least landed safely without injury. All's well that ends well.

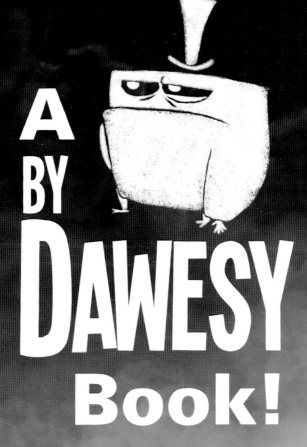

A
BY
Dawesy
Book!

Mind-Boggling Mini Masterpieces

Ten Tiny Tales

Volume 1

Written and created by

OLIVER DAWES

Illustrated by Snej Mommsen

ISBN 978-1- 9162615-1-8

First published in the UK 2020

www.bydawesy.com

Printed and bound in the UK

THE PIG

Dr Fitzpattenburg was a genius. To most, she was the smartest Earthling ever created, trusted, tried and true. She had engineered a way to save the human race. Time was running out and soon the aliens would come. Their threat to human existence was terrifying. With no option to relocate planets – proving a logistical nightmare – Dr Fitzpattenburg's new shrinking machine meant she could recolonise eight billion Earthlings by injecting them into a single pig. Aliens would have no business with a pig. Oinkington, Snoutsville, Bacon Village and Trotterstown were a few of the suggestions for new areas people could live within The Pig.

Of course, there were protests, alternate proposals, failed scientific solutions and mass hysteria meltdowns … but with the aliens coming and time running out, The Pig was the only option. And so, inside The Pig the humans hid.

Years went by, but the aliens never came. It was a great big stinking lie. Dr Fitzpattenburg made it up! She just didn't like humans and she quite fancied living on planet Earth all by herself. So, once every last being was injected into The Pig, Dr Fitzpattenburg decided not to follow, instead, be alone, a planet of her very own, just her and her pet pig Chopsywopsy.

Sometimes Dr Fitzpattenburg would whisper into Chopsywopsy's ear, "I am God now."

The End

SILENT
SKIN-SHELLS

The sun is shining, I sit outside, I sip my coffee and watch the world go by. But this isn't a world you know. What wanders by isn't warm and fleshy, but cold and floaty. Maybe I should have moved away by now? But I love this coffee shop and I love my home. Not many people stay in the same town for more than a year, it freaks them out, seeing themselves walking by. A ghost from their past. But not me, I quite like it. I find it fascinating watching who I was last year …

What do I mean you must wonder? In my world we shed our skin. Every year when the sun sets on the thirty-first day of the twelfth month – a Silent Skin-Shell leaves our body.

For the rest of time it elegantly and gracefully follows the same path it did that year on a silent rotation over and over. So, if you stayed in the same place for thirty years, you would likely see thirty copies of yourself individually living their lives as you did each year – The ghosts from your past.

Most people can't live in the same home for very long. They would have to live with their ghosts. Millions build their own small hut every year because older homes already contain countless ghosts of other people – walking around, repli-cating their past lives. The problem is, space is running out, and the Silent Skin-Shells are now everywhere. There are so many the air is almost filled with a fog. A thick fog of ghosts from our pasts. But I like it, I like watching the Silent Skin-Shells and I particularly enjoy spot-ting my old self.

Sometimes I'll say something like, Oh look, it's me from three years ago, I remember that time, that was the day I went into the green grocers and bought a watermelon. But today I get it wrong; I see myself, but not happily gallivanting with a watermelon. I watch as I cry in the street. That was the day my pet Capybara was sick so I took it to the vets. That was a really sad day. I tried to move on, but now I remember. Maybe it's time for me to depart this town, and leave my ghosts behind.

The End

MR GRUMPY BUTTERCUP

The legend is true. If you hold a buttercup under your chin, the beautiful yellow petals will tell you whether or not you like butter by shining a glorious golden glow, or not, against your skin to confirm your buttery status. In a small village called Churnsville, a miracle graced the flowing pasture. It was the biggest buttercup you ever saw – its stem as strong as a tree stump, its petals brighter than the sun. People came from all over the globe to visit the giant buttery bloom – to show off to their foes a selfie or three with the magnificent flower. But there was one old man who disapproved, a grumpy old soul who lived alone in a single house on top of a hill overlooking the enchanted cup. He tutted and shook his head at the tourists – mumbling profanities as he passed them daily. But one day there was shocking news. The buttercup was gone and the miracle was missing. But it didn't take long to figure it out – the grumpy old man had stolen the prize for himself. But, not in anger, in hope instead – according to the police report here's what they said.

This grumpy old man who hated butter, once had a wife who loved it so. She was called Margarine and their lives were perfect until one day she had to leave him. He found out soon after she couldn't bare to be with a man who despised her passion. The grumpy old man was bitter for years until one day he snapped and stole that cup. He knew it was powerful but what happened was completely unexpected. He assumed such a powerful buttercup would change his hate to love and his darling would return, if only he held its muscular stem and alluring petals under his chin all night long. But instead, as a cheesy full moon graced the skies and the dairy gods spoke, a yellow beam struck his chin and his blood turned to butter. So much so, his body exploded and buttered his walls like an inviting slice of a seeded batch.

The news spread and his wife arrived. The police said, "Don't look," but she burst on in. She wasn't shocked or upset. But, instead, pulled a croissant from her jacket pocket, grabbed a handful of buttery blood and slapped it on her pastry. She then whispered to Mr Grumpy Buttercup, "Oh, I love you now."

The End

LIAM COPPERDALE

Door to door sales was Liam Copperdale's profession. He was magnificent – possibly the best in the country. He was a very handsome man but he worked differently to others. He didn't believe in using his good looks to make a sale, so instead wore a paper bag over his head. Taking a sneak peek out of the window or through the spy hole was enough to put someone off opening the door to Liam Copperdale as they were scared. But, caught unaware and opening the door without pre-warning meant many were stood face to face with a bagged Liam Copperdale and didn't want to close the door in case they seemed rude.

When Liam Copperdale did have the opportunity to sell face to face, or face to bag, bag to face (but never bag to bag) he had a 100% success rate! Why you may wonder? Because Liam Copperdale sold high tech home security systems that meant opening the door to a man with a bag on his head could quickly become a thing of the past.

The End

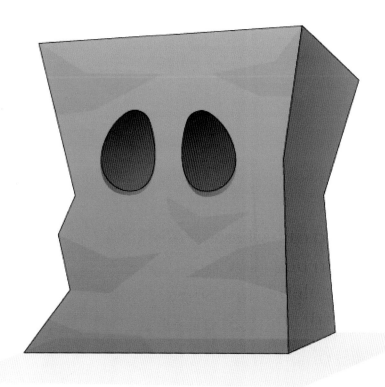

THE FARM SHOP

Mrs Saddlehurst ran a farm shop in the middle of nowhere. No one ever came as the shop smelled of pee. People wondered how she managed to keep things afloat with no custom. But, there was one man that came at the end of every week. Mrs Saddlehurst would keep the shop open Monday-Saturday 09:00-17:00 and on a Sunday 10:00-16:00, yet the man would only ever visit at 15:55 on a Sunday. He would leave with a small jar covered by a brown paper bag. The rest of the week, not a single soul would visit her shop.

Health and safety visited the lonely shop one afternoon and immediately closed it down. The shop only contained jars, hundreds of jars and nothing else. They removed the contents for further testing, concerned at what they'd found. Here's a list:

Goats pee ultra 250mls & 500mls
Goats pee ultra with added saliva 750mls

Pigs pee maximum force 250mls & 500mls
Pigs pee mega mix 150mls

Cows pee supreme 250mls
Cows pee extreme power 500mls

Chickens pee ultimate premium 50mls
Chickens pee superior slushy 20mls

The man had read the local newspaper and was sad to see that health and safety had closed the farm shop down. The following Sunday, as usual, the man visited the shop at 15:55 and read a sign in the window which confirmed the news: 'closed until further notice'. He posted a letter through the door, lightly placed his palm on the door, and then walked away.

Later that evening Mrs Saddlehurst opened the letter and read it out aloud …

Dear Mrs Saddlehurst,

I'm sorry to hear your shop has been shut down, but I'm glad we did business for so long. Although your prices were extortionate – especially the 'Pigs pee mega mix' at an eye watering £8,000 for 150ml, I can assure you, although the health and safety laws are strict in the UK, my sell on fee of £18,000 in Oysterland has been a revelation. Over the course of twenty years whilst we have been doing business, Big-Oyster-Pharma now fully validates that rubbing the ointment into ones face does prevent aging. It's a shame our trading has ended and for now the Oysterlandians will have to age naturally. Let's wait until the dust settles and then maybe talk business again …
In the meantime, I have enclosed a cheque to reimburse any losses until we meet again.

To Mrs Saddlehurst
£2,700,000
Igor Oysterhoft

The End

PHOTO BOOTH

The walls of East Netherington were huge and heavily guarded by robots. Without explanation residents could never leave and outsiders could never enter. It had been this way for hundreds of years. The residents had everything they needed – medical assistance, supermarkets, entertainment and homes, but no information or contact with the outside world. On one street stood an old, weathered photo booth. It wasn't plugged in, but every now and then, electrical sparks jumped around it, over it and inside it. Rumours over the years was that if you sat inside the booth it would steal your soul … so from a young age the photo booth was the thing of nightmares.

Every now and then someone would enter

enter that booth – perceived as either insane or too brave for their own good. When you live in a world where you know no different, you tend to 'monkey see, monkey do'. But sometimes you're just born different. Well, that was the view of the government anyway, that's how they decided who would make the cut. Whenever someone did enter the photo booth, as they exited, they were never the same again – they were a shell of their old self.

The government enjoyed the photo booth process. It would steal the mind of whoever sat inside and transfer it to their computer system which would then determine if that person was either crazy or brave. If they were crazy, their mind would be deleted, and if they were brave, their mind would be added to a robot body to live on the outside world as a humanoid. This is why anyone who went into the photo booth came out brain dead. Their minds were stolen!

With a pent up civil war on the horizon due to disputes lasting over one-hundred years between the two remaining colonies on the planet, the government was using East Netherington as a farming plant to produce the bravest humanoids possible to win a war should it break out. The process continues …

The End

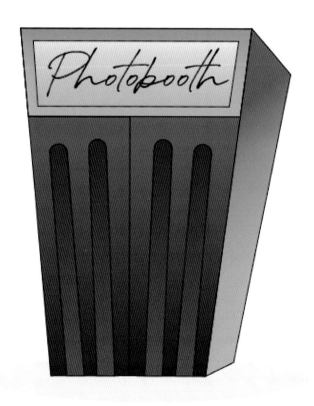

I-SCREAM

The I-Scream van was running low on
stock, so a visit to the mortuary was in
order to replenish the goods. As soon as
Dr Bambagoosga knew the coast was
clear and skeleton staff were working –
usually around 3am – she would sneak
into the mortuary with her large bag and
stock up on blood treacle, liver slithers,
bone cones and wrinkle sprinkles. She
wasn't proud of what she did, but she
wanted an early retirement. Being a
Doctor paid well, but not as well as the
freaks that desired her gruesome treats –
those who liked a little extra on their
I-Scream.

She would drive her I-Scream van while
the stock was fresh and deliver in the
dead of night, usually around 4am to a

pre-arranged location. So, if your loved one ever mysteriously leaves the house around 4am, and has a hankering for the unusual – maybe, just maybe, they're visiting the I-Scream van for something a little more scary than dairy …

The End

THROUGH THE GLASS

The year was 2100. People had become lazy, unmotivated, morbidly obese, too tired to move and too stubborn to change.

A fixed benefit to survive was transferred into the accounts of those that didn't want to question the system and were happy to just exist on a quick blast of serotonin delivered via gluttony. The thirst for adventure was no more, but the thirst for sugar was at its peak. Travel was a thing of the past. People were glued to their sofas. They could order any calorie they desired, delivered by drone into their snack hatch like a privileged rabbit hutch. They stare into their screens with an unlimited amount of sugar-coated, brainwashing TV – so much had been produced over the past two-hundred years that there was enough on screen entertainment to keep you glued for one hundred lazy lifetimes. They were set for life. Eat, watch, sleep, repeat. No need to leave the house. For the few in control, big business was in window TVs. You could buy a window package which meant you lived anywhere in the world from the comfort of your own chair. Take a look outside … Monday: mountains with wonderful waterfalls. Tuesday: tsunamis that couldn't destroy your home, a thrill to be had! Or perhaps a weekend away … Saturday and Sunday: sunny beaches, wicked waves and beautiful blue skies. No need to leave your house.

The glass is cold to the touch, but warm to the soul and hot to those in control. No need to leave your house. No need to buy a door. Spend it on a window TV instead and lose yourself through the glass.

The End

CRUMBS

Sweep, sweep, sweep, scoop, scoop, scoop, pour, pour, pour and sleep, sleep, sleep. This was the daily routine of Agathoramax, a huge but gentle monster that lived on Earth.

Agathoramax didn't like the other monsters, they were mean and relentless. They would eat whatever and whoever stood in their way – swipe, crunch, swallow and repeat. But the crumbs, oh the crumbs! Agathoramax would despair. What a mess those awful monsters would leave – on every surface, remains of their meals left to rot.

Agathoramax was a beautiful soul, she did not take pleasure in eating the same foods as the other monsters, and certainly did not like cleaning up after them. But how was Agathoramax supposed to enjoy living on Earth unless the human crumbs were swept up. Remove the reminder, remove the smell, one day it may stop and she can wave farewell! The other monsters certainly wouldn't do it. So left to Agatho-ramax it was.

If she stopped, she would become over-whelmed, if she kept going, she could hope it would end.

So she would grab her broom, frown upon those human crumbs – sweep, sweep, sweep, scoop, scoop, scoop, pour, pour, pour then sleep, sleep, sleep.

The End

STONES

Whenever Griffin Rhodes got out his pouch of coins to pay for something, people would point and laugh. Not because he had a pouch, but because when he poured his coins into his hand, four precious stones would nestle neatly in his palm. People would ask, "Why? What's a man to do with random stones?"
Griffin would gently reply, "I quite like them, they make me feel good. Besides, I've had this feeling for a while, a deep fulfilling feeling I'm supposed to carry these stones." But, people would shrug and repeat that same old question, "What's a man to do with random stones?"

One dark winter's morning, Griffin Rhodes awoke from a very deep sleep. He opened the curtains and squinted his eyes.

Something was unusual, something was different. He placed his hand on the window and felt heat, a heat unknown to a winter's morn. Then a flash of lightning, but none like he'd ever seen. The colour was curious, it was neon green. As quick as a flash, to find out more, he put on his trousers and was about to exit the door. One last stretch, his arms reached up high, when all of a sudden the roof ripped into the sky. A demon swooped in and grabbed Griffin Rhodes by his out-stretched arms. He screamed so loud but felt it was too late.

As the demon held him in its hand, Griffin could see right across the land. There were other demons with humans in their hands, all begging for their lives, trying to pay their way out. Griffin pleaded, "Where am I, what do you want?" The demon replied, "You're on the other side and eat you I will."
"But wait, I can pay, I can give you whatev-er you want." The demon laughed and

explained money was of no use. Griffin pulled out his pouch and placed his four stones between the giant demons fingers as he was being held tight, "I have these," he whispered, losing breath. The demon's eyes widened at the sight of the precious stones. He dropped Griffin and swallowed the majestic gems. Griffin fell to his bed and bumped his head on the wooden bed post. He stood, then walked slowly to his window. He placed his hand on the glass – it felt cold. He was home.

The End